Little Vera

KINOfiles Film Companions
General Editor: Richard Taylor

Written for cineastes and students alike, KINOfiles are readable, authoritative, illustrated companion handbooks to the most important and interesting films to emerge from Russian cinema from its beginnings to the present. Each KINOfile investigates the production, context and reception of the film and the people who made it, and analyses the film itself and its place in Russian and world cinema. KINOfiles also include films of the other countries that once formed part of the Soviet Union, as well as works by émigré filmmakers working in the Russian tradition.

KINOfiles form a part of KINO: The Russian Cinema Series.

1 *The Battleship Potemkin*
   Richard Taylor

2 *The Man with the Movie Camera*
   Graham Roberts

3 *Burnt by the Sun*
   Birgit Beumers

4 *Repentance*
   Josephine Woll and Denise J. Youngblood

5 *Bed and Sofa*
   Julian Graffy

6 *Mirror*
   Natasha Synessios

7 *The Cranes are Flying*
   Josephine Woll

8 *Little Vera*
   Frank Beardow

9 *Ivan the Terrible*
   Joan Neuberger

10 *The End of St Petersburg*
   Vance Kepley, Jr

LITTLE VERA

FRANK BEARDOW

KINOfiles Film Companion 8

I.B. TAURIS
LONDON · NEW YORK

Published in 2003 by I.B.Tauris & Co. Ltd
6 Salem Road, London W2 4BU
175 Fifth Avenue, New York NY 10010
www.ibtauris.com

In the United States of America and in Canada distributed by
St. Martin's Press, 175 Fifth Avenue, New York NY 10010

Copyright © Frank Beardow, 2003

The right of Frank Beardow to be identified as the author
of this work has been asserted by him in accordance with the
Copyright, Designs and Patents Act, 1988.

All rights reserved. Except for brief quotations in a review, this book, or any part thereof, may not be reproduced, stored in or introduced into a retrieval system, or transmitted, in any form or by any means, electronic, mechanical, photocopying, recording or otherwise, without the prior written permission of the publisher.

ISBN 1 86064 611 5

A full CIP record for this book is available from the British Library
A full CIP record for this book is available from the Library of Congress

Library of Congress catalog card: available

Set in Monotype Calisto by Ewan Smith, London
Printed and bound in Great Britain by MPG Books Ltd, Bodmin

Contents

List of Illustrations	vi
Acknowledgements	vii
Note on Transliteration and Translation	viii
Production Credits	ix
Plot Synopsis	1
Introduction	3
1 The Historical and Political Context	10
2 Analysis	13
3 Themes	56
4 *Little Vera* and the Soviet Youth Film	94
5 Reception	97
6 Concluding Remarks	108
Further Reading	113

List of Illustrations

1	Map of Ukraine.	5
2	The opening panoramic shot of the town.	14
3	Vera destroys the 20-dollar note.	19
4	Fishnet stockings.	24
5	Vera and Chistiakova at the disco.	25
6	Sergei on the prowl.	26
7	Vera puts Father to bed.	29
8	Sergei enters the café.	30
9	The barge party.	32
10	Viktor pontificating.	33
11	The special lunch.	37
12	The sex scene.	38
13	Airport farewells.	40
14	On the beach.	43
15	Sergei hurts Vera.	44
16	Chistiakova and Vera in the kitchen.	45
17	Vera sobbing at the table.	46
18	Sergei loses his temper.	47
19	Father consoles Vera after the picnic.	50
20	The attempted rape.	52
21	Vera with photograph and sparklers.	53
22	Final scene on the sofa-bed.	55
23	Mother's hands.	76
24	The tiger.	85
25	The goods train.	91

Acknowledgements

I am grateful to the University of Sunderland for granting study leave in the autumn of 1999 to begin work on this book and to the Centre for European Studies for a travel grant which enabled me to visit Moscow in January 2000.

My thanks go to family and friends, colleagues and postgraduate students. I should like to single out Leonid Iliushin, Manuela Lühmann, Thorsten Mack, Nina Mileshkina and Stephen Torgersen; Martin Dewhirst, Stuart Parkes and Deborah Thomas; Paul McNab, John-Paul Green, Sarah Gillighan and Darren Connor. An immense debt of gratitude is owed to Alexander Pozdniakov at Lenfilm, particularly for providing contacts and helping with copyright issues. Maria Khmelik and Vasili Pichul were kind enough to answer queries. The final responsibility for all flaws in interpretation remains, of course, mine alone.

Thanks also to the Inter-Library Loan Service, Learning Development Services and my School's Technical Services at the University of Sunderland. Bloomsbury Publishing kindly gave permission to quote from letters in the appendix to Maria Khmelik's novel *Little Vera*. Illustrations from the film are courtesy of Vladimir Grammatikov, chief executive officer, and Elena Smirnova, senior consultant, at Gorky Film Studio and Alexander Aizenberg, editor-in-chief at Krupnyi Plan Video Productions. Finally I am indebted to Richard Taylor and Philippa Brewster for their advice, comments and patience.

This book is dedicated to the memory of my parents.

Note on Transliteration and Translation

Transliteration from the Cyrillic to the Latin alphabet is a perennial problem for writers on Russian subjects. I have opted for a dual system: in the text I have used the Library of Congress system (without diacritics), but I have broken from this system (a) when a Russian name has a clear English version (e.g. Maria instead of Mariia, Alexander instead of Aleksandr); (b) when a Russian name has an accepted English spelling, or when Russian names are of Germanic origin (e.g. Yeltsin instead of Eltsin); (c) when a Russian surname ends in ii or yi this is replaced by a single y (e.g. Dostoevsky instead of Dostoevskii), and all Christian names end in a single i. In the scholarly apparatus I have adhered to the Library of Congress system (with diacritics) for the specialist.

All translations are my own, unless otherwise stated.

Production Credits

Production
Director: Vasili Pichul
Screenplay: Maria Khmelik
Director of photography: Efim Reznikov
Editor: Elena Zabolotskaia
Art director: Vladimir Pasternak
Costume designer: Natalia Poliakh
Make-up: Valentina Zakharchenko
Music: Vladimir Matetsky
Sound: Pavel Drozdov
Assistant director: Valentina Pereverzeva
Lyrics: Igor Shaferan ('Your Voice'; 'It's So Good')
Camera operator: B. Filimonikhin
Story editor: Vera Biriukova
Production unit manager: Iuri Prober
First assistant cameraman: E. Liubinsky
Assistant editors: Elena Semenovykh and Sofia Iaroslavskaia
Stunt co-ordinator: N. Sysoev
Colour: L. Redulesku
Release year: 1988
Production company: Gorky Film Studio
Country: USSR
Running time: 129 minutes (Russian version); 119 minutes (USA)

Cast

Vera: Natalia Negoda
Sergei: Andrei Sokolov
Father (Nikolai/Kolia): Iuri Nazarov
Mother (Rita): Liudmila Zaitseva
Viktor: Alexander Alexeev-Negreba
Chistiakova (Lena): Alexandra Tabakova
Andrei (Andriusha): Andrei Fomin
Tolik: Alexander Mironov
Mikhail Petrovich: Alexander Lenkov

Supporting cast
A.Vasilev, G. Goriachev, V. Zakharchenko, E. Mariutina, G. Mitrushina, E. Fishkina, M. Khmelik, Natasha Smeian, Maxim Nairabe

Plot Synopsis

Vera lives in a run-down, provincial, industrial town with Kolia, her long-distance lorry-driver father whose sole relaxation seems to be the bottle, and Rita, her care-worn mother, who works shifts as a production quality controller at a local factory. The family lives in an unprepossessing block of flats. Vera has an unhappily married brother called Viktor, a self-seeking doctor in Moscow. Vera, who has just left school, has reluctantly applied for a place on a telephone operators' course at a local trade school. Vera and her friends, the wayward Lena Chistiakova, the part-time currency speculator Tolik, and the aspiring naval cadet Andriusha, idle away the summer with the help of alcohol. Rita, worried about Vera's behaviour and believing that Vera always had a special relationship with Viktor, asks the latter to come home to help Vera mend her ways. In the meantime Vera, much to Andriusha's chagrin, falls for the handsome, aloof, engineering student Sergei, whom she meets at a local open-air disco. Sergei has the reputation of being a sexual athlete. Although Lena is interested in him, he spends the night with Vera in the student hostel where he lives. Andriusha leaves for Naval College. Vera's behaviour continues to annoy Kolia, who persists in seeking release through alcohol and nostalgic songs. Lena begins an affair with Mikhail Petrovich, a middle-aged divorcee. Viktor arrives from Moscow and mouths platitudes. Vera is not impressed. Viktor, it transpires, knows Sergei. Viktor, while womanising and drinking at the hostel, discovers Vera in Sergei's room. He is enraged. Sergei claims that he wants to marry Vera. Vera agrees, though Viktor warns her of his reputation. The news of the marriage is not welcome at home. Vera tells her mother that she is pregnant, which is untrue. She asks her to tell Kolia. Nevertheless the family arrange a special meal to celebrate the engagement. Sergei arrives, shocking Vera's parents with his outlandish and inappropriate Bermuda shorts and T-shirt. Although Sergei is polite, Viktor warns his parents that it is all a sham. Sergei then upsets the family by walking out and taking Vera with him. Subsequently, Vera, while making love, chides Sergei for his bad behaviour. She also tells him of her lie about being pregnant. Viktor's return to Moscow means that there is a spare room at home. Without further ado, she and Sergei move in with her parents. The relationship between father and prospective son-in-law continues to deteriorate. Matters come to a head at Kolia's birthday party, which Sergei reluctantly attends. Sergei, provoked by Kolia, locks him in the bathroom. When Vera eventually lets him out, Kolia stabs him with a kitchen knife. Sergei is rushed to hospital. Viktor is once again summoned from Moscow. His solution is to prescribe tranquillisers. Vera is persuaded by her mother to change her earlier statement to the police and to suggest that it was Sergei who had provoked the father. Vera, dismissed by Sergei, bumps into Andriusha who is home on leave. He tries to force Vera to have sex with him. She fights him off. This is the last straw for her. She tries to commit suicide. Sergei discharges himself from hospital, meets up with Viktor and they both arrive back at the flat to be confronted by Vera's suicide attempt. Viktor saves her. He then tells his parents to look after her and satisfactorily to resolve the investigation into the stabbing as he has to return to Moscow. While Sergei and Vera sit together on the bed and wonder what the future holds for them, Kolia has a heart attack in the kitchen and dies.

Introduction

What's sensational about [the film] is that there's nothing sensational in it.[1]

Vasili Pichul and Maria Khmelik, director and screenwriter of *Little Vera*, are a husband and wife team. Vasili Pichul, the son of a blue-collar worker from Zhdanov in Ukraine, was born in 1961. From 1977 to 1983 he studied in Marlen Khutsiev's workshop at VGIK, the All-Union State Cinema Institute. Maria Khmelik was also born in 1961. Her mother, Rosa Perez, had been evacuated to Moscow during the Spanish Civil War. She subsequently married the playwright Alexander Khmelik. Maria Khmelik studied at VGIK in Evgeni Gabrilovich's scriptwriting workshop.

The following instructive exchange with Pichul appeared in *Cahiers du cinéma*, a leading French film journal, in 1990:

> *Cahiers*: You have the advantage of being young and making successful cinema at a unique moment in the history of your country. What store do you set by the great venture of Soviet cinema, Dziga Vertov and the others?
> *Pichul*: I was never interested in those films. They bored me. Nowadays I appreciate their aesthetics. On the other hand, I sympathise with the fate of Vertov as one of many human beings crushed by that totalitarian machine.
> *Cahiers*: Which films inspired you to become a film-maker?

Pichul: None. I lived in the provinces ... What drove me to become a film-maker was the overwhelming desire to change my life. I was very young then and it seemed to me that only cinema could offer me this chance. It was only after I had entered VGIK that I watched films.[2]

If Pichul feels no indebtedness to classic Soviet cinema, then where does his inspiration for film-making lie? At VGIK it was Hungarian cinema that made a great impression on him, primarily the work of Márta Mészáros. The daughter of the sculptor László Mészáros, she was born in 1931 and brought up in the Soviet Union. Her father disappeared in the gulag. She studied at VGIK and her films were instrumental in helping Pichul's generation to formulate a film language of their own.[3] Her first feature film, *The Girl* [Eltávozott nap, 1968] was the story of a young orphan who traces her mother, only to be rejected. However, it was *Adoption* [Örökbefogadás, 1975] that was her first real success. This unsentimental film told the story of the problems confronted by Kata, a widow in her early forties who wants to have a child. Other films were *Nine Months* [Kilenc hónap, 1976] and *The Two of Them* [Ök ketten, 1977].

Since their student days Vasili Pichul and Maria Khmelik have collaborated as film-maker and scriptwriter. *Little Vera* was their debut feature film. In 1983 Maria Khmelik visited her husband's home town, which has reverted to its former name of Mariupol, for the first time. It is a grim industrial town, polluted by iron and steel and coke and chemical works. For her diploma project at VGIK she wrote a script which drew on her impressions of this visit.

Pichul and his wife, eager to make the most of *glasnost*, reworked this script and between 1983 and 1986 they offered it to every Soviet studio producing feature films in Russian. They met with no success. Although the studios all thought highly of the script, they felt that it would never be approved. Eventually, Tatiana Lioznova, a well-known film-maker and also a high-ranking state official, sensing that the atmosphere was changing in the Soviet Union, gave it the green light. Pichul, however, was determined to make the film *his* way.[4]

Maria Khmelik later told an American journalist that she had written the screenplay as 'a biting indictment of the misery to which the "heroic proletariat" was consigned by the Soviet leadership'.[5]

Vasili Pichul, on the other hand, was slightly more charitable. 'The film is an attempt to come close to the abyss of our life today,' he told an American film scholar. 'Actually,' he continued, 'our life is even darker, and yet I remain an optimist. Making a film is an exercise in hope.'[6]

Pichul commented that, in private, some members of the government disapproved of the film and requested that the number of copies for distribution be limited.[7] According to Andrei Plakhov, a leading film critic, one of the reasons for the disapproval may well have been the film's sexual explicitness.[8] An *Izvestia* article declared that the

1. Map of Ukraine.

film was problematic because it conveyed a gloomy picture of the life of ordinary people.⁹ Pichul won through none the less, claiming in the *Cahiers du cinéma* exchange that 'some intelligent people were found' to persuade the government officials to change their minds and to make available 1,600 distribution copies.

Anne Williamson, an American reviewer, alleges that the Moscow authorities declined the invitation to send *Little Vera* to the Cannes Film Festival in the spring of 1988. She also alleges that there were rumours to the effect that influential directors were intriguing against the film at the time. Included among them was the prominent filmmaker and actor Nikita Mikhalkov, who was later to have such box-office successes as *Burnt by the Sun* [Utomlennye solntsem, 1994] and *The Siberian Barber* [Sibirskii tsiriulnik, 1999].¹⁰ However, I have not been able to substantiate these allegations.

This Companion to *Little Vera* aims, first, to furnish non-specialists with sufficient political and historical background for them fully to appreciate the film. It is axiomatic that all artefacts are products of a particular environment and a particular time. The action of *Little Vera* refers to the period in the Soviet Union known as the 'era of stagnation'. Yet at the same time the appearance of the film in 1988 reflected the spirit of openness that characterised Gorbachev's early years in power. 'The era of stagnation' has become associated primarily with Brezhnev. By the end of the Brezhnev era, desire for change was in the air and Gorbachev capitalised on this. His policy of *glasnost* actively encouraged freedom of expression in the arts and the media. Heated discussions took place about the Soviet past and present. Cinema played an important role. There were re-evaluations of the past in formerly shelved films such as Abuladze's *Repentance* [Monanieba, Russian title Pokaianie, 1984] and Askoldov's *Commissar* [Komissar, 1967] or in new films such as Proshkin's *The Cold Summer of 53* [Kholodnoe leto 53-go, 1987]. In *Little Vera* neither the older generation nor the younger generation lives up to the official image promoted by the state.

It has been argued that *Little Vera* exemplifies '*chernukha*', a term that can be applied to art, literature or film. Deriving from the word for 'black', it means the representation of the dark, the negative, the seamier side of life. In their book *The Zero Hour*, Andrew Horton and Michael Brashinsky proposed six criteria for a *chernukha* film: the collapse of the family; immorality and unmotivated cruelty among average Soviet citizens; the death of former ideals; cramped living conditions; senseless hysterics; and 'adult' scenes.[11] Although *Little Vera* fulfils most of these criteria, it has a lighter side to it, which prevents it from belonging to the classic *chernukha* film genre. It might be more appropriate to suggest that the film exemplifies '*novyi realizm*' (new realism), a sort of Soviet-style neo-realism.

The second aim of this book is to analyse the film's major episodes. I have tried to act as a sensitive guide, sharing my thoughts, concerns and enthusiasm with the viewer as we explore the film's narrative.

The third aim is to deepen appreciation of the film by concentrating on three of its themes. We begin with *byt*, a Russian term meaning everyday life, not some state-promoted, ideal image of the life of its citizens, and we focus on certain 'spaces'. By 'spaces' I mean the sites where this life is enacted, both at the macro-level and the micro-level. Macro-level spaces represent the external, official world: industrial complexes, transport facilities, educational institutes, civic institutions, housing and leisure facilities. Micro-level spaces represent Vera's world: the various rooms in her parents' flat; the flats of her friends; her lover's hostel room; and the places where she 'hangs out'. The spaces are not always what they seem.

We then pass on to the theme of progressive alienation by concentrating on 'bundles of relationships', that is, contrasting families and family relationships, and varying degrees of friendship, from school pals through close personal friends to suitors and lovers. I want to show how these spaces and bundles of relationships contribute to Vera's suicide attempt.

Finally we examine the theme of cycles as suggested by the opening and closing panoramic shots of the industrial landscape and the symbol of the goods train which moves back and forth across the screen several times during the film. In the light of the ambiguous ending of the film, I speculate about Vera and Sergei's future life.

The fourth aim is to place the film in the context of Soviet 'youth film'. Jūris Podnieks' ground-breaking film *Is It Easy to be Young?* [Legko li byt' molodym?] appeared in 1987. It was this film which paved the way for films like *Little Vera*.

The final aim is to acquaint the viewer with both Soviet and Western critical reaction to the film. This ranges from ordinary newspaper readers' letters and the views of the film's leading actors to mainstream criticism.

In 'Letters from a Bag', Maria Khmelik wrote:

> It seemed to me as though all these letters were written by my characters. Here are Vera's parents, outraged by teenage promiscuity. Here are her friends, some of them desperately struggling to find their way in life ... Here is Vera herself, and Sergei. And here are the neighbours in their five-storey rabbit warren: the workers, pensioners, teachers and doctors, the medalled veterans, the truck-drivers, the housewives ... [T]hese letters [gave] me a glimpse of the terrible loneliness in which so many of these people live.[12]

Little Vera has been described as 'the first ever Soviet sex film'. Many readers' letters expressed disgust at the depiction of the sex act and particularly of the sexual position adopted, whereas the Western film publicity machine sought to exploit this one scene in order to entice the general public into the cinemas. However, both attitudes are misleading. The sex scene occupies only 1 minute and 20 seconds of the film's 129 minutes. It is in no way titillating. Rather, it is an important indicator of the state of the relationship between Vera and Sergei. To see it otherwise is to do a disservice to the director and the scriptwriter.

Not surprisingly, most Western and Soviet reviewers and critics tend to focus on the film's historical and sociological significance. Examples of such criticism are offered, but, for the sake of completeness, other approaches with different emphases are also mentioned.

If this companion to *Little Vera* encourages viewers to watch the film more than once, then it will have succeeded in its aims. *Little Vera* deserves to be viewed for the right reasons.

Notes

1. *Dumaite o reklame* [Think about Publicity] 4, Moscow (1988), p. 24.
2. 'Cine-perestroika: le rideau déchiré', special supplement, *Cahiers du cinéma*, Paris (18 January 1990), p. 26.
3. Information received by the author from Vasili Pichul and Maria Khmelik.
4. *Cahiers du cinéma*, op. cit., p. 25.

5. Hedrick Smith, *The New Russians*, London, 1990, p. 111.
6. Andrew Horton, *Film Quarterly*, 13, no. 4 (1989), p. 21.
7. *Cahiers du cinéma*, op. cit., p. 25.
8. *Sight and Sound*, no. 2 (1989), p. 83.
9. *Izvestiia*, 4 March 1989. This article is cited by Dmitry Shlapentokh and Vladimir Shlapentokh in *Soviet Cinematography 1918–1991. Ideological Conflict and Social Reality*, New York, 1993, p. 181.
10. Anne Williamson, 'Rubles of the Game', *Film Comment*, January–February 1989, pp. 23–6.
11. Adapted from Andrew Horton and Michael Brashinsky's *The Zero Hour: Glasnost and Soviet Cinema in Transition*, Princeton, NJ, 1992, pp. 163–4.
12. Maria Khmelik, 'Letters from a Bag', appendix to *Little Vera*, London, 1990, pp. 117–18.

1. The Historical and Political Context

Little Vera is very much a product of its time, of the *glasnost* era. That its script had lain untouched since it was written in 1983 is not surprising, given its content. Brezhnev died in November 1982. His successor, Andropov, died two years later and *his* successor, Chernenko, one year after that. Brezhnev's legacy had been economic stagnation, corruption in high places, a decline in moral standards and the war in Afghanistan. Andropov had reintroduced discipline and tried to eliminate corruption. Chernenko's reign was too short-lived to make any impact.

Gorbachev and some of the more progressive-minded Party members who had been waiting in the wings now realised that their moment had come. Gorbachev was elected General Secretary in March 1985. The so-called Soviet Spring arrived a year later. *Glasnost* allowed for greater freedom of expression. Literature became a critical force, calling for a reassessment of the past and its relationship with the present and the future. However, most critics agree that, of all the arts, it was cinema that played the most substantial role in supporting the directives of the Twenty-seventh Party Congress in February 1986. Cinema took *perestroika* (restructuring) and *glasnost* to heart, and, indeed, turned them to its advantage. In May the Fifth Congress of the Union of Cinematographers voted out the once liberal, but now conservative Kulidzhanov (First Secretary), Karaganov (the board's secretary) and 75 per cent of the old guard, including the privileged film-maker Nikita Mikhalkov. Elem Klimov was elected First Secretary and was joined on the board by such respected or progressive directors as Vadim Abdrashitov, Eldar Shengelaia and Andrei Smirnov, and the film critic Andrei Plakhov.[1] In December, Goskino (the State Committee for Cinema) was restructured, its arch-conservative and Brezhnev-appointed minister, Ermash, being replaced by the younger Alexander Kamshalov.

The first act of the newly elected Board of the Union of Cinematographers was to establish the so-called Conflict Commission, chaired by Plakhov, to review and reinstate 'shelved' films, that is those 1960s and '70s films which had been banned by Goskino, often on dubious grounds. Among the films released were Kira Muratova's *Brief Encounters* [Korotkie vstrechi, 1968] and *Long Farewells* [Dolgie provody, 1971), Alexei German's *Trial on the Road* aka *Road-check* [Proverka na dorogakh, 1971] and *My Friend Ivan Lapshin* [Moi drug Ivan Lapshin, begun in 1979], Andrei Mikhalkov-Konchalovsky's *The Story of Asia Kliachina Who Loved but Did Not Marry* [Istoria Asi Kliachinoi, kotoraia liubila da ne vyshla zamuzh, 1966], Tengiz Abuladze's *Repentance* [1983–84], which was to become synonymous with *perestroika*, Alexander Askoldov's *Commissar* [1967], Sergei Paradzhanov's *The Legend of Suram Fortress* [Legenda o Suramskoi kreposti, 1984], Gleb Panfilov's *Theme* [Tema, 1979], Alexander Sokurov's *The Solitary Voice of a Man* [Odinokii golos cheloveka, 1978], Boris Frumin's *Errors of Youth* [Oshibki iunosti, 1979] and Elem Klimov's *Agony* [Agoniia, 1975], *Farewell* [Proshchanie, 1981] and *Come and See* [Idi i smotri, 1985].

The Fifth Congress had also singled out problem areas in the cinema: the poor quality of film criticism in the specialised journals, technical backwardness, the failure to cultivate younger talent, and the far from satisfactory mechanism for distribution. A five-day workshop, organised by Klimov, preceded the 1987 plenary session of the Cinematographers' Union. There, according to Anna Lawton, 'directors, screen-writers, critics, film theoreticians and sociologists played a game in which they shifted roles with each other (distributor, producer, editor etc). The purpose was to work out a *new model* for cinematography.'[2] At the plenary session Klimov called for a radical overhaul of the film industry. This was the beginning of a new approach to film production and distribution. New Model Cinema was to be independent and to move towards self-financing (*khozraschet*).

Younger film-makers now had a chance to show their talents. The results were impressive. In 1987 Jūris Podnieks completed his examination of the alienation of youth, *Is It Easy to be Young?* This was followed in 1988 by Marina Goldovskaia's *Solovki Power* [Solovetskaia vlast], a stunning documentary about the northern gulag. A series of feature films that might be placed in the category of 'Coming to Terms with the Past' included Proshkin's *The Cold Summer of 53* (1987) and Abuladze's *Repentance* (released 1986).

Little Vera was in at the very start of *perestroika*. Taking full advantage of the spirit of *glasnost*, it set about debunking many of the cherished myths of the Soviet Union, the family, the working class and youth.

Notes

1. For details see Ian Christie, 'The Cinema', in Geoffrey Hosking and Julian Graffy (eds), *Culture and Media in the USSR Today*, London, 1989, pp. 44–5; and Anna Lawton, *Kinoglasnost: Soviet Cinema in Our Time*, Cambridge, 1992, pp. 53–7. Both critics suggest the possibility of guiding hands from on high.
2. Anna Lawton, 'New Model Cinema in the Soviet Union', *Soviet Observer*, 15 January 1988.

2. Analysis

Title and Panorama

Immediately we are informed of the identity of the heroine of the film. This is Little Vera's story. Yet we wonder why the adjective 'little' is applied to her. The significance of both the adjective and the heroine's given name will become clear only at the end of the film. The sound of waves washing along the shore is the first indication of the location. The music begins eerily, serving as an accompaniment to a panoramic shot of what at first glance resembles a camp in the manner of the opening shot of Caspar Wrede's *One Day in the Life of Ivan Denisovich* (1970). Gradually our attention is drawn to the emissions from some sort of furnace against a night sky. In the left-hand corner in blue appear five names, one after the other: Natalia Negoda, Liudmila Zaitseva, Andrei Sokolov, Iuri Nazarov and Alexander Alexeev-Negreba. Although we subsequently learn that these are the actors, there is no reference to the roles they are playing. Only Zaitseva and Nazarov would be well known to an older generation of Soviet film-goers. Nor do we have the usual convention 'A film by...'. In fact, at first sight, we could be dealing here with a documentary. The film stock lends a grainy quality to the picture, thus adding to this impression. When the second name appears, the music becomes more lyrical. This will eventually become the theme tune for Vera, her signature tune, which functions rather like Lara's theme in David Lean's *Doctor Zhivago* (1965).

The fade to daytime reveals a panoramic view of an industrial

14   Little Vera

2. The opening panoramic shot of the town.

landscape. If the previous night-time sequence had been evocative of Soviet industrial power, working through the night to fulfil production targets laid down by Five-Year Plans to bring about all the more swiftly the Bright Future of Communism, then in the second shot things are seen in the cold light of day. These dark chimney stacks emit fumes, pollute the atmosphere, stunt the greenery and choke the workers who live in the drab, identical, high-rise apartment blocks. This is everyday reality. The birds' twittering and a lone bird call seem muffled, too. The theme of nature and its destruction by man is thus underlined.

Exposition

The camera picks out the bottom half of a goods train as it makes its way towards a crossing. We assume that this train comes from one of the many nearby industrial plants we have seen in the opening sequence. The train is empty, but whether this is significant is unclear at this stage. At any rate, its presence reinforces the town's insularity. Such trains are functional, serving local industry. There is no indicator of another reality to which to escape by passenger train. We shall notice how many times this goods train appears in the course of the film. Little details, like the shafts of strong sunlight or the dust thrown up by a lorry, establish the season: summer. The waste ground, where the lorry comes to rest, suggests the run-down state of the area. From the driver's clothes we deduce that he is an ordinary worker. His language, too, reinforces this impression. The very first expression he utters is 'Damn it!', though the original Russian is stronger, something like, 'It's enough to make me spit!' A contradiction is implied. The man does not fit the stereotype of the 'glorious worker' promoted by the state; he seems more concerned with the safety of the brown paper-covered bottles rattling in his string bag.

Cut to a medium close-up of a young woman standing on a balcony eating cherries. Different cultures view things differently. To an English-speaking person, a bowl of cherries is something pleasant (the expression 'Life is a bowl of cherries' springs to mind). In Ukraine, where the film is set, cherries are sour and, although they feature as fresh fruit, compôte or preserves or even as dried fruit for pies, they are also used as a common cure for a hangover. The young woman has no make-up. Her hair is still wet, presumably from the shower, yet it is lunchtime. Has she had a late night? Our attention is drawn to her nondescript dress, torn at the back, which she has not bothered to mend. Her sunglasses might well be fashionable in the provinces, or so she believes, but they look cheap. The balcony is the first of the private spaces we encounter. It affords some escape from the cramped conditions of the flat, but there is little room to sit, just enough space for a couple of chairs. A pop record blares out in the background. On the surface, this pop song, like many of the everyday details we shall encounter, is simply part of the narrative. The young woman, having purchased this current hit, seems preoccupied with its catchy melody. However, the title – 'Summer is Over, as If It Had Never Been' – alerts us to the song's underlying meaning: the impermanence of feelings and the harshness of reality, which will become themes of the film.

Cut to the kitchen, where the lorry driver's wife prepares his lunch. This is the main meal of the day, hence the tomato soup, rissoles and fried potatoes. Again the hand-held camera picks out everyday details in a fly-on-the-wall manner. Note the wall-mounted radio receiver. Through such receivers the state could control the flow of information, as the single frequency carried only approved broadcasts. Although many citizens at this time had access to multi-frequency radio sets, they were far less common in the provinces. The innate conservatism, even the backwardness, of the provinces is alluded to here.

The camera focuses on the wife's hands, as if to underline her function as constant provider of meals. The camera brilliantly catches the cramped conditions. When it tracks back, it is as if there is not enough room for it; it is almost squeezed out by the couple. Her simple, brown and white floral dress, her standard, tight perm, are indexes of the working class, while also pointing to restricted choice. The significance of the contents of the husband's string bag becomes clear. He has managed to get hold of some bootleg alcohol. Drink, or alcohol abuse, will be a leitmotif of the film. He is so preoccupied with siphoning the alcohol that he does not listen to a word his wife says. Actually they do not speak normally, they yell at each other. We also note that the wife's first words are to criticise the behaviour of the young woman, their daughter. She manages to blame both the school system and her husband. His 'Yeah, yeah' suggests that this is not the first time he has heard these reproaches. At no stage in this scene do husband and wife refer to one another by given names. The daughter is referred to as 'she'. This gives the impression of dulled sensitivity, of coldness in the relationships, or it points at the very least to an unhappy family atmosphere.

After the first outburst there is a return to a normality of sorts with an inquiry about lunch, but the wife soon finds another opportunity to voice her dissatisfaction with her husband. He does nothing around the house and, despite frequent requests, has failed to mend the bathroom light. She then suggests contacting Viktor, their son. Only when the father yells 'Vera!' do we identify the young woman on the balcony as the heroine of the film's title. The father's angry 'Am I talking to myself?', his irritated switching off of the record player and his aggressive arms-akimbo stance are almost parental clichés. We have the first indication of the theme of the dysfunctional family and the generation gap.

Cut to the balcony. The father brushes through the bamboo curtain to confront Vera who continues to ignore him. The bamboo curtain with its exotic palm trees manages to be both naff and ironic. It recalls far-away places, sandy beaches, swaying palms. It is out of place in this working-class environment. This family has no chance of visiting such a place. It is tempting to suggest that the bamboo curtain represents an attempt to individualise the flat, to compensate for its drabness. It is more likely, however, that a consignment of such merchandise had just happened to become available in the shops. Its effect is rather like the 'flying geese' on Hilda Ogden's wall in *Coronation Street*, the long-running, working-class, British soap opera. The difference is that Hilda Ogden had a choice. For Vera's mother, it is this or nothing.

We note that Vera's hair has dried out sufficiently to reveal highlights. Is this a sign of youthful rebellion? (Remember her mother's ultra-conservative hair-do.) The father now decides on a different tack and begins to address Vera in a much gentler tone, though it does not last long. Nevertheless, the gentler tone suggests a special relationship between father and daughter. His 'what-will-people-say?' attitude reveals much about his character and at the same time points to the village mentality among the many families having to live in such cramped, drab blocks of flats. The father's understanding of a daughter's allotted role is clear: mother's little helper. His unfavourable reference to Chistiakova, Vera's friend, introduces the theme of friendship that will be developed in various forms in the course of the film.

The parental tirade continues in the kitchen. Vera brushes past her father for the second time.

Back on the balcony his final appeal to her conscience is phrased in terms of a contrast between Vera's selfishness and the parents' self-sacrifice. From the balcony to the kitchen and back, the father moves from the generalised 'we' to the more personalised 'your mother and I'. He refers to his wife and himself as a normal couple with normal concerns and expectations. Most parents can identify with these sentiments. Yet we note that his arms are still akimbo and he loses further sympathy by introducing his son into the equation. Though his utterance may be translated as 'Thank God Viktor has made something of himself', his actual words in Russian are: '*Viktor stal chelovekom*' [Thank God Viktor has become a man]. It means that Viktor has found his place in society, something which, sadly, Vera has patently not done. Interestingly enough, the father does not say that Viktor has become 'a Soviet man'. There were many popular slogans glorifying Soviet man: 'Man of Labour'; 'Man is a Friend, Comrade And Brother'; 'Man – How Proud It Sounds' ['*Chelovek truda*'; '*Chelovek cheloveku drug, tovarishch i brat*'; '*Chelovek – eto zvuchit gordo*']. In the film there is very little reference to official ideology, except for the cynical attitude of the younger people towards it, as we shall see.

The father's sights are set lower. Viktor has a wife, a son and a responsible job. The father exaggerates the knock-on effect: Vera's behaviour could easily prejudice her brother's career. On the other hand, the mother's interjection about smoking, though more prosaic, is risible. Smoking pales into insignificance beside other probable activities. When the father directly demands an answer and points his finger aggressively at Vera, her reply ('What is there to say?') betrays an indifference that manages to be insolent at the same time. These are the first words Vera utters in the film. They suggest, 'I don't want to talk about it. You've said it all. Your minds are made up.' This signals a classic, generational breakdown in communication. When the mother speaks, she continues to scold her daughter. The insistence on enlisting Viktor's help does, however, point to some sort of special relationship between older brother and younger sister.

Cut to Vera's bedroom, one of the few private spaces available to her. The posters stuck to the wall are standard teenage paraphernalia. Most are of male pop stars or film stars: Nikolai Eremenko, the son of an equally famous crooner, The Harrays, a Swedish pop group, and Viktor Tsoi, the rock legend and film idol. Some of the posters are taken from *Sovetskii ekran*, the very popular but less than glossy film magazine. It is all rather tacky, like Vera's life. The sellotape from one of the posters has come unstuck and the poster flaps in the draught. There is another telling detail: the doll perched on top of the lamp is a reminder of a more innocent and happy time in Vera's life, though it looks as if it might fall off at any moment. Vera, if we believe her parents, has already fallen.

Even on the telephone the mother's voice is strident. She asks if she is through to Moscow. The Soviet telephone service was unreliable, so she checks that she is through to the right place – another authentic touch. She addresses Viktor's wife as Sonia, her son as Vitia, diminutive forms of Sofia and Viktor respectively, terms of

3. Vera destroys the 20-dollar note.

endearment. The mother's stridency disappears once she begins to talk to her grandson Misha. Her use of Russian is uneducated. She makes the common mistake of misplacing the stress on the verb 'to telephone'. She also uses the slang term for a 'call'. Her conversational range parallels the limits of her own life – family, weather and food. She treats family members as consumers of food that she provides, in this case, fruit for little Misha. The interjections 'Ah ha' and 'Mm' suggest that she uncritically accepts Sonia's brief explanations for not keeping in regular contact. As soon as Misha comes on the phone, the mother's tone softens even more. The effect is greater because her words are spoken in a voiceover while the camera focuses on Vera. This conversation may well remind the mother of bringing up her own children. Camera movements heighten the tension. During the phone call there is a close-up of Vera nonchalantly eating her cherries in her room. This is replaced by a close-up of the frown on the mother's face as she gets down to the business in hand – Vera's behaviour. The mother had come across a 20-dollar note in Vera's bag; Vera merely claimed to have found it in the street. It is as if Vera no longer exists as a person in her mother's eyes; she has become an object. Even when we do see Vera in the background, she is out of focus.

This constant undermining of a daughter by both parents can easily lead to psychological trauma. The mother's change of tone once again emphasises how serious the matter of the dollars is. It is as if she has been woken from the idyllic world of bringing up children to the harsh reality of coping with an adolescent. The mother presents the facts to Viktor and, by extracting the offending 20-dollar note from her pocket and brandishing it in the air, she seeks to impress on Viktor the gravity of the situation. It is a futile gesture, of course, since he cannot see it. Even when she speaks of the money, her poor education betrays her. 'Twenty *foreign* dollars' she calls them. The mother is portrayed as a law-abiding citizen. She had advised Vera to go to the police, yet, as we shall see later, she has double standards when the law affects her and her husband. When Vera rushes from her room and snatches the note from her mother, the camera has difficulty in capturing the moment and is forced to get out of the way, thus underlining once again the pressure-cooker atmosphere of living cheek by jowl. Note that the mother calls her Verka, a diminutive that would normally be used with a naughty child. Vera's tearing up the note and flushing it down the toilet is a clear act of defiance, if not a challenge. As the mother reports this and other acts of defiance, her brow becomes even more furrowed. She stares fixedly at Vera, who has been varnishing her nails in readiness for a night out on the town, a clear indication, in her mother's eyes, of wanton behaviour.

However, Vera now stands beside her, almost dwarfing her, eloquent testimony to Vera's having won the first round on points, as her laconic replies to Viktor confirm. One final detail: there is a sort of wall hanging above the telephone, a white, line drawing of a naked woman on a black background. The depiction is within the bounds of decency. Such hangings were popular at the time. It is unclear whose idea it was to buy such an item, though we might speculate that it was the mother's choice, after having been assured by friends at work that it was in good taste. I shall return to her reliance on the advice of friends later.

We are now given a brief view from the balcony. Once more we get an idea of the limitations of Vera and her parents' world. The blocks of flats have few amenities. A single communal swing is visible. The passing, empty goods train suggests routine and parallels the monotony and emptiness of the parents' lives. Just as they follow their routine, going to and from work each day, so the train fills up at the plant, dumps its shoddy load and returns empty, only to fill up again and repeat the process.

The father enters through the bamboo curtain, picking his teeth with a matchstick, and carrying an unlighted cigarette in his hand. The use of the matchstick as a substitute for a toothpick is spot-on. As he looks momentarily to the left, he spots a little boy on the swing. Perhaps he, like his wife earlier, is momentarily reminded of happier days with his own children. Vera's reply to his question about Viktor's advice is wonderfully ironic. She cannot resist the opportunity to have a dig at her father as he draws on his cigarette. 'Don't smoke!' she says. 'And listen to your parents!' She does not listen to them, they do not listen to her and they do not listen to each other. The father quotes a proverbial saying, 'Guard your honour from youth'. The commonsense moral attitude expressed in the phrase would be in line with his upbringing and his value system, so out of date for Vera's generation. Times have changed. The reference to 'honour' (virginity) is not lost on Vera. When the mother joins them on the balcony, she asks if everything is OK. Ironically, the word used in Russian means 'normal'. Can what we have witnessed so far be regarded as normal? I shall return later to this phrase.

The mention of a letter from college fixes the time of the exposition: the period between leaving school and entering further education. Vera has applied to a PTU, a vocational-technical institution or trade school, which trains semi-skilled workers for dead-end jobs. Perhaps the father is ignorant of the fact that in such institutions standards are low and students poorly motivated. This is hardly an encouraging prospect. In the course of the exchange Vera just looks bored and checks whether her nails are dry. Yet her father prizes education. He is pleased that Viktor has become a doctor. It is only natural that he should want his daughter 'to make something of herself'.

The exposition has determined the parameters of the narrative in terms of genre, setting, themes, tone and initial relationship-bundles. *Little Vera* is a youth film. The setting is delineated by the opening establishing shots at night and the following morning: a coastal town, dominated by industry, its working-class inhabitants incarcerated in drab, five-storey blocks of flats. The goods train's progress emphasises the monotony of life. The polluted landscape sets up a contrast with 'the glorious achievements' of Soviet society. This illusion/reality principle will be highlighted in the course of the film. The film moves from general to the specific space. The immediate focus of attention is one particular, working-class family and its problematic relationships, the generation gap, alienation, as well as questions of friendship. The characters do not talk; they yell and bicker. Their speech is markedly working-class, uneducated. The use of grainy film stock (possibly poor quality) contributes to the film's realistic, gritty tone. The employment of fly-on-the-wall techniques adds to the sense of confinement and entrapment. The camera gets in the way of the characters, as they get in each other's way. This is life in your face.

The Saturday-night Hop, Provincial Style

The open-air disco near the park is one of the few municipal amenities. It is pretty uninspiring, resembling a circus arena, with fairy lights and a gaudily painted perimeter fence. It is patrolled by police with Alsatian dogs. This police presence is disturbing. There was a period in the 1970s when the authorities used members of the Komsomol (Young Communist League), in disguise, to patrol, monitor and, if necessary, to break up youth concerts where the music was considered 'ideologically harmful'. Here, however, the police presence may be to pre-empt trouble. We have just witnessed the narrow escape of Tolik, a friend of Vera. The disco has not really started. That is why we hear pre-recorded Soviet pop music in the background. We notice, too, that several girls wait, alone and bored, on the benches. There is little to do in such towns. The disco is one of the few '*tusovki*', places to hang out. At this stage there are only seven girls and Vera and her friend Andriusha, thus the impression is given that the police authorities may have over-reacted.

Our attention is immediately drawn to Vera's dress. In complete contrast to the torn dress she had worn at home, here she has dolled herself up. The result is a mixture of sensuality and tartiness. She rests her elbows on her knees, a classic teenage slouch. Andriusha's clothes are designer-label, an indication of social class. Vera's clothes are a sign of teenage rebelliousness, of the need to assert her individuality as well as to counteract the drabness of her everyday life.

We deduce from the respective positions that they occupy on the bench – Andriusha slightly further forward than Vera – that their relationship is strained. Furthermore, for much of the dialogue, Vera refuses to establish eye contact with him. Andriusha's nervous diffidence is seen before his first words. It is as if he is trying to summon up the courage to make a move. Vera's replies are terse; 'Where to?' or 'What for?', for example. When he proposes that they go to his place, her reply suggests that she is aware of his ulterior motive. Andriusha's ploy is banal, though he thinks that he can impress her with the foreign tapes he has 'acquired'. In Russian the verb 'to acquire' implies difficulty in obtaining and is frequently used for items in short supply or from abroad. We later learn that his father is in the navy, a job which affords him access in foreign ports to goods that would be largely unobtainable at home. Vera uses Lena Chistiakova as her excuse. Three may be a crowd in Andriusha's eyes, but Vera is not keen to be alone with him. His reaction suggests that it is not the first time that the 'Chistiakova card' has been played. Although Vera slightly softens her tone when he mentions his call-up papers, his 'I have to go away soon' irritates her. It is one of the oldest tricks in the book, a pretext for getting her into bed. She sees through it. Andriusha seems fond of her and he meets her irritation with a smile. Vera looks away, ignoring him. Is she just bored by him? Is she unenthusiastic about a possible future with him? Could she do better? The way she flicks off her cigarette ash lends support to all these interpretations.

Tolik appears. He is self-confident, physically fit and proud of it. Vera likes his style. Notice the way she willingly goes off with him to the dance floor. They have their arms around each other's waists. Tolik's French patter, which consists of the odd phrase culled from a school textbook, is simply awful, though he has probably impressed the local girls with it before. Tolik loses his 'Mr Cool' image over the missing 20 dollars, which belong to another, more highly-placed gang member nicknamed Chika, who is also known to Vera. We begin to feel uneasy about some of the company she keeps. Tolik seems less attractive when we realise that he has used Vera and, by hiding the money in her handbag in an attempt to save his own skin, has turned her into an accomplice. Tolik then becomes aware of the presence of the rival gang at the disco and dashes off to defend his turf.

Cut to Vera and Andriusha sitting in exactly the same position as before. Vera keeps him in the dark about the conversation with Tolik. She either ignores events or plays them down. It is a form of denial, an attempt to avoid reality. We wonder how such an attitude will affect her in the future.

Cut to a medium shot of the disco in full swing. Vera is joined on the dance floor by Chistiakova. They seem like girls out for a good time. Note the change in Vera: she has suddenly come alive.

Cut to a tall, good-looking, fair-haired young man. He is given his own 'frame', as if to emphasise his importance in the unfolding story. There is an immediate contrast with Andriusha and Tolik. Andriusha, despite his designer-clothes, seems like 'the boy-next-door', and Tolik 'the boy-from-the-wrong-side-of-the-tracks'. Everything about Sergei (we learn his name later) is cool – looks, hair, stylish gold chain and pendant, blue denim shirt. The matchstick between his teeth reminds us of Clint Eastwood or his cowboy loner character; he is certainly film-star material. The way he moves, however, spells danger. He does not walk, he prowls, his eyes seeking out

4. Fishnet stockings.

Analysis 25

5. Vera and Chistiakova at the disco.

attractive females. Is there any wonder that Andriusha feels compelled to place a protective arm over Vera's shoulder to assert his territorial rights? Both Chistiakova and Vera are impressed by this newcomer. Note, however, the way the camera homes in on Vera's face when Sergei comes across. It is as if he is trying to eye her up. He may well have made a mental note of the protective arm but he is sure of himself. Chistiakova responds first. There is something desperate about her willingness. Sergei is only too happy to demonstrate his 'pulling power'.

Cut to two rival gangs lined up on the dance floor (shades of *West Side Story*). A cut to the police taking a break heightens the tension, the lull before the storm. A close-up of the gun holster of one of the policemen hints at the possibility of violence. The back-up van and reinforcements suggest that this is not the first time that they have been called in. It is a pattern. The replacement of Komsomol activities and recreational pursuits provided by the state in palaces of culture by gang warfare is not to be tolerated. Vera seems to enjoy the fracas and she can certainly take care of herself. The police brutality is disturbing, their grinning faces showing that they are just as bad as the youths. The disco is one of the few amenities available, yet it is

6. Sergei on the prowl.

turned into a brawl, exacerbated by the police. Have these young people become so disaffected that brawling has become a ritual, a way of bringing a bit of excitement into their lives?

Getting to Know You

Vera, who is sitting alone on a wall in the harbour area, whistles to attract Sergei's attention. He joins her. We wonder why, after the fracas, Vera did not just go home. After all, she has ended up on her own. The prospect of another row with her parents would probably be too depressing. Though she sits smoking, she does not seem to be enjoying the cigarette. It is less a way of asserting her independence, more just something to do, to relieve the boredom. When Sergei asks her her name, he immediately uses the familiar form of address. This '*ty*' form in Russian is the equivalent of the French '*tu*' or the German '*du*'. Vera follows suit even though they have only just met. This easy familiarity would be frowned upon by her parents' generation.

Sergei's self-assuredness is evidenced by his directness in referring to Chistiakova as 'a cow'. Vera admires his guts. She tells him that she and Chistiakova are like sisters. 'All people are brothers and sisters,' he replies with a laugh. His remark is ironical, bordering on cynicism. It was a slogan invented by the regime to maintain the myth that Soviet republics and satellite countries were equal partners, irrespective of national and ethnic differences. Aware of the double standards that apply, he adds: '[B]ut some get their faces bashed in.' His self-assurance is further exhibited in his next actions – taking Vera's cigarette and the masculine display of his crotch. Apprised of Vera's view of her relationship with Andriusha, he proceeds to the attack. He can take Vera, but the way he squeezes her cheeks is disturbing. He does not seem averse to inflicting pain. Vera does not like it. However, Sergei is so sure of himself, he knows that she will not be spending the night on the bench. The intonation of his 'Oh, really?' makes that clear.

How was It for You?

Sergei was right. He knew that Vera would come back to the student hostel with him. Let us note first of all the authentic details of the room. It contains two iron bedsteads, a cupboard-cum-screen, table and chairs, institutional-green, tatty walls and old-fashioned radiators. There has been an attempt to personalise, to individualise it: a cardboard tiger, a commandeered railway sign, a collection of cigarette packets fixed to the back of the door. The room is only a semi-private space – the second bed indicates that it is normally shared, so the other occupant has probably gone home for the vacation. The tiger triggers off a series of associations: we have already seen Sergei *on the prowl* at the disco; is the tiger a present from his fellow students who are aware of his sexual conquests? His tactics are stalking his prey, picking them up, plying them with alcohol – note the bottle of cheap champagne and the two glasses on the table – loving them and leaving them. Is he so cynical, we wonder? There is, after all, a certain veneer of politeness about him in that he offers to see Vera home.

However, we cannot fail to make a mental note of the long hesitation before he answers Vera's question, 'Do you love me?' What is going through his mind? Is this a one-night stand or could the relationship be worth pursuing? His reply, when it does come ('Of course!'), leaves his options open while at the same time it reassures Vera. Her sigh is one of contentment. Let us also note that on her way out Vera deposits the champagne bottle with the other empties beside the door. How many times has she done this at home? It is conditioning.

In vino veritas

The dining room. The camera tracks back and down from a string of 'sunflower' fairy lights between wall lamps to reveal the father slumped in a chair, in his vest and trousers, smoking and listening to a drinking song performed by Vladimir Vysotsky, the bard of his generation (1938–80). This major episode fleshes out the state of family relationships. It is confrontational and follows a pattern – quiet, crescendo, quiet. All is not as sunny as the fairy lights with their smiling 'sunflower' faces suggest. There is a line in a popular Soviet song 'The March of the Aviators' which ran: 'We were born to turn the fairytale into reality!' The father seems to reverse this ideal. He is quite happy to get drunk and listen to his favourite songs. Vera towers above the slumped figure, as if she is the parent and he the child. Just as she had tidied up at Sergei's, so too, here. She also prepares something for her father to eat. His maudlin sentimentality is answered with weary resignation or by an effort to humour him. She has heard it all before. His reminiscences about being put to bed drunk by Vera in the past are a cause for concern. 'Mother will read the riot act' is Vera's way of suggesting 'Be a good boy!' The parent/child reversal continues. She switches off the music. Later he switches it back on. At first the voices are quiet. The father, for all his brashness, misses his grandson. That is why he is so upset to have learned that Viktor will be coming to visit alone. It is Vera who mentions Viktor's wife. She seems to have sussed that Viktor's marriage is not working out.

Tempers flare when the mother arrives home. Note that at first the father is referred to simply as 'he', just as the parents in an earlier scene referred to Vera as if she did not exist. At first the mother elicits some sympathy. Having finished her shift, she has also done the shopping on the way home, the usual experience for women in the Soviet Union. She wants to avoid a scene. 'Kolia, keep your voice down. P-l-e-a-s-e,' she implores wearily. This is the first time we have

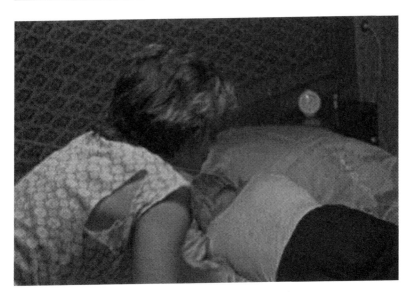

7. Vera puts Father to bed.

heard her call her husband by his given name. We feel that she, too, is talking to a child. Kolia is the alcoholic 'baby' who needs to be looked after. Vera and Mother merge into one.

An abrupt change of tone is triggered by Vera's innocuous reference to the father's razor being on the balcony where it usually is. Yet he takes this as a slight. He does not command respect; he *demands* it. His idea of nurturing is the heavy hand; children need to be thrashed. He attributes his daughter's sluttishness to her mother. Capable of giving as good as she gets, the mother merely replies that Vera is his daughter as well. She and Vera have heard it all before. His mood swings are typical of a drunk, from maudlin sentimentality to rudeness and finally to self-pity. Vera has no option but to treat him like a baby. She is fully aware that his problem is drink-related. She is caught between her parents. According to them she should be the dutiful daughter. Had not her father earlier asked why she did not help about the house? Now her mother complains that she has not washed the floor. She expects Vera to deal with her drunken father when the occasion demands and does not even thank her.

8. Sergei enters the café.

Café Nondescript

Vera and Chistiakova meet up over ice cream and coffee. The café is another public space that is less than appealing, with its boringly repetitive 'Muzak'. The fact that there are only four customers speaks for itself. The waitress is not even visible. Vera is wearing her disco outfit again. They speculate about the relationship between a middle-aged man and a young girl sitting at a nearby table. Vera is shrewd enough to guess that the man is divorced and that the girl is his daughter. Chistiakova asks Vera whether she will write to Andriusha at Naval College, thus revealing her traditional attitude to romance.

Sergei appears, framed in the doorway *à la* Clint Eastwood. His designer stubble adds to his allure. Chistiakova is bowled over. Her expression, 'He gives me a buzz, like a boa constrictor with a packet of insecticide', became a catch-phrase among young people. Having learned that Sergei is more attracted to Vera, she gives vent to her irritation with the words, 'I can see the beginning of a [B]right Soviet feeling'. The irony would not be lost on a Soviet audience, for they would see a parallel with the phrase 'the Bright Future of Communism'. Chistiakova's decision to turn her attention to the divorcé reveals both shallowness and an eye to the main chance. She is desperate for a husband.

Situation 'Normal'

Night. The goods train clanks its way across the screen. Cut to the kitchen where the camera picks out dried fish and assorted jars before taking in Vera as she washes up. Mother comes in, tired out and out of breath from carrying shopping bags. They decide to go to bed. The bathroom bulb blows. The mother reprimands Vera again for not washing the floor. This little scene encapsulates what we have learned so far. The goods train parallels the monotony and futility of life in the town. There is the mother's double burden: it is midnight when she gets home after completing her shift and the shopping. By providing the dried fish, usually eaten with beer, she effectively colludes with her husband over his drinking. Mother's and daughter's roles are confirmed. Note, too, that the mother has to use a vaporiser for her asthma, which is exacerbated if not caused by the pollution. The mother is obsessed by food: her job is to provide it, the family to consume it. Father does nothing around the house. The bathroom light is still faulty. Mother scolds Vera again.

The Drunken Farewell Party

Friends gather at Andriusha's parents' well-appointed flat. Although Andriusha's mother approves of Vera, the latter makes it clear, at least to Andriusha, that their relationship is going nowhere by bursting out laughing when he tries to grope her. The real farewell party takes place on a barge on the docks, away from this non-working-class, conservative environment. The friends join in the 'down-the-hatch' drinking ritual. Vera becomes progressively more inebriated, as if to blot out reality. She fails not only to recognize Mikhail Petrovich, the divorcé from the café, who suddenly arrives with a bouquet for Chistiakova, but also to realise that the flowers are not intended for her. The action unfolds in such a way that we come to observe the subtle changes in the relationships. In the flat Vera and Chistiakova had sat together, Andriusha apart. On the barge Tolik, the fixer, the clown and the cynic, abandons Vera as soon as he realises that she will probably not intercede with Chika. Chistiakova has come to accept Vera and Sergei's relationship and now seems prepared to settle for second-best with the conservative Mikhail Petrovich. Andriusha still refuses to give up his pursuit of Vera. His doglike devotion extends to his doggy paddle after his dive into the sea. In the end he resembles a pitiful, bedraggled dog. Our final impression is of an environment wrecked by pollution, its young inhabitants by alcohol.

Vera staggers off to Sergei's hostel where she tries to re-enact the balcony scene from *Romeo and Juliet*. We wince. The lovers are second-rate. The roles are reversed. The courtly apartment is replaced by the hostel, Verona by Mariupol. The ladder, left behind by a workman, is rickety and there are two requests for a helping hand. The lines of the declaration of love are drunkenly fluffed. Despite all of this, we do not doubt Vera's passion and vulnerability. A few chords from 'Vera's theme' accompany the declaration, adding poignancy and tenderness to the scene, as if to underline the genuineness of her emotion. In her eyes Seriozha, as she affectionately calls him, is extraordinary.

9. The barge party.

10. Viktor pontificating.

The Return of Big Brother

We are introduced to a little more of the town's landscape as we accompany Vera and her father to the airport to collect Viktor. Vera, still wearing her 'gear', looks exhausted and constantly yawns. We know why. Father's insults are consistent. Whereas he was drunk the first time he called her a slut, this time he is sober. The effect on the viewer is all the more shocking, though it does not worry Vera unduly. She is so used to it that it has become a meaningless ritual and, as usual, she ignores it at first. She 'plays' at the breath-test her father inflicts on her. She has the moral high ground. He *demands* to know what she has been up to, just as he *demands* respect as a father. Note the question 'Am I talking to myself?' This is the second time we have heard this typical parental cliché.

Cut to a close-up of Viktor. We notice that he is smartly dressed. No one speaks. He stares ahead at the road, the scene a far cry from what he has become used to in Moscow. He reluctantly admits his marriage problems, though in Russian his expression betrays more: 'We've decided not to get in each other's way.' Whereas Vera is quick to understand the concept of trial separation, their father does not.

He resorts to criticising Vera. Viktor does not intervene. 'Vera's theme', which began this drive back home, has been progressively drowned out. Note how the father refers to Vera as 'she'. Viktor's observation is telling: 'Here we go again!'

Cut to matching cabinets and photographs of Viktor and Vera as children. These photographs, which have pride of place, are a poignant reminder of a time of innocence. But what has Viktor grown up to be? A pontificator. 'A child in the family isn't just an object that has to be disciplined or ordered about all the time,' he declaims. It's all rhetoric, as if he is quoting from a Soviet textbook. Vera laughs raucously. Compared with his speech, her laugh is genuine. Remember how she laughed at Andriusha's farewell. Her laughter cuts through the nonsense as does her interjection, 'He doesn't believe those things he's saying. You don't either.' The mother can only resort to a 'your-elders-know-better' attitude. Viktor is closer to his parents' value system than he would care to admit. Note that once he has made his speech, he sits down. He has done his bit. He can now help himself to his father's homebrew and his mother's meal in his honour.

Big Brother's Double Standards

Sergei sits, bare-chested, eating tuna out of a tin and drinking a Pepsi. Unlike the rest of Vera's friends, Sergei is not a drinker. We notice for the first time a third bed, a wall-bed. Once the vacation is over, Sergei will have to share with two other students. Vera arrives and it is not long before they move to the bed. When Vera says that she loves him, he exclaims, 'Hurrah!' The use of the expression may be ironic, but we momentarily question the genuineness of his feelings for Vera. A drunken student enters without knocking and demands a tin opener. Someone sings in the background, 'Why do all the girls fancy him? That's the secret.' The singer is Viktor who now enters, inquiring 'Where's our tiger? Where's this hostel's throbbing sexual pulse?' Viktor confirms our impression of Sergei. His song establishes Sergei's reputation, and the equating of the tiger and the sexual pulse reinforces it. He elaborates on this by reading aloud from the AIDS leaflet pinned to the wall, as if it refers to Sergei's life of dissipation. Viktor, too, is no stranger to fooling around. He has just slipped away from a party and from the company of an attractive female medical student who now appears. The difference is that Viktor is married. We suspect that this is not the first time he has played away from home.

Reluctantly, Sergei comes from behind the screen to greet him. When Vera suddenly slinks in, the camera remains on Viktor's stony face for a few seconds. He is as shocked by her behaviour as he is by the fact that he has been caught out. However, he immediately takes the high moral ground. It is his duty to protect his sister's honour! Note Vera's ironic repetition of the phrase, 'All people are brothers and sisters', that Sergei had used when they first met. Viktor addresses Vera as if he were a father chastising a daughter. Stunned by Sergei's almost casual remark about wanting to marry Vera, Viktor issues the standard warning about men like Sergei. He then decides that the best course of action would be to call Mother at the factory. Note that he uses the formal 'Mother', not 'Mum'.

Viktor leaves. We are left to wonder why Sergei mentioned marriage. Was it just a spur of the moment decision? We become even more concerned when we hear his vision of married life. It is nothing more than a set of clichés: Vera waking up and seeing him beside her, Vera cooking nice meals for him. What a self-centred, male-chauvinist view! Vera, however, really wants to marry him. The die is cast.

Here We Go Again!

Stripped to the waist because of the stifling heat, the father and the son sit at the kitchen table. The father is clearly drunk – there are at least six bottles of beer on the table. The father does not eat, he just drinks, a bad sign, a portent of confrontation. Viktor reverts to his provincial ways, rather uncouthly biting off chunks of bread. Father begins to taunt Vera. His speech is full of impotent rage and his language is vile. He calls her 'you dockside whore!' Vera, as usual, does not respond. She seeks refuge in her bedroom, where, as if to prove to herself that she is no whore, she admires herself in the mirror. To the father's demand to know where the 'bastard' lives, Viktor replies that he does not know. That elicits a grin from Vera, since she knows that he does not want to implicate himself. Note that he remains silent after this. The father yet again reveals his fear of losing face with the neighbours. His self-pity changes to aggression with his final outburst: 'Aren't we good enough for you, you bitch?' He fails to see that he and his wife are flawed.

Slightly Pregnant

Vera tries to soft soap her mother so that she will persuade her father to let her marry Sergei. Vera's mother's view of marriage in general is jaundiced but ingrained; she has been conditioned by *her* mother. Love disappears after the honeymoon to be replaced by drudgery, cooking and clearing up after the man. Although she advises Vera to get an education, she still approves of the traditional roles of females. This becomes clear after Vera alleges that she is pregnant. She asks her whether she wants a boy or a girl. 'A boy!' says Vera with conviction. 'Fool!' exclaims her mother. She herself had wanted a girl who would help her with the housework.

Meeting the Future In-laws

The scene is prefaced by a view of the empty goods train clanking across the screen and of the communal swing on which a child sits, supervised by his parents. It is a scene of happy family life in the sun, an ironic comment on what is to follow. The last time we saw the swing there was a child and only one parent. We recall that Chistiakova is the daughter of a single mother. Her own boyfriend is now a single father. Viktor may well end up in the same boat.

The importance of the meal is marked by the use of the dining room. Wonderful food has been prepared, largely by the mother, we suspect: salads, duck, aubergine, wine, champagne and proper vodka. Mother and Vera wear outfits that we have not seen before. Even the father has been cajoled into dressing for the occasion. Yet the atmosphere is tense. Father swears, 'Where's that damn fiancé of yours?' He even orders Viktor to stop whistling. Vera and her mother are on edge. Once Sergei arrives, the introductions are formal. The father gives his name and patronymic, though the mother tries to break the ice – 'Auntie Rita ... Rita'. This is the only time her name is used in the film. Given the effort the family has made, Sergei's 'gear' seems even more out of place. Viktor, though he is fully aware that Sergei is playing games, remains silent for a long time.

Analysis

11. The special lunch.

Vera's father is true to form. He cannot wait to crack open the vodka. Sergei is over-polite, affecting a formal style: 'One is studying. Then one intends to devote oneself to one's chosen profession and, of course, to one's dear family.' Yet, beneath this veneer, he is poking fun at Vera's parents, particularly at her father's drinking habits and lack of savoir-faire. Note his patronising, 'We forgive you, don't we?' Mother is also true to form, deferring to Sergei's superior knowledge of wine etiquette. Father's phrase, 'Forward, singing!' is worth commenting on. It alludes to the custom of marching and singing in official parades in honour of communism. We may recall this sort of marching in musical films of the 1930s. Father, however, has reduced the slogan to a vulgar toast. Soon the other family members revert to their 'normal selves'. Brother and sister have a slanging match. Mother acts as mediator.

When Sergei abruptly announces his and Vera's departure, their reactions are as expected. Father is more concerned about the booze, Mother about the food. Vera is confused. Viktor's half-suppressed laugh confirms that he knows Sergei only too well. 'Well, we met him!' says the mother in a voiceover. Sergei's behaviour has prepared the family for what is to be expected from him in the future and they will have to get used to it, for Vera's sake. On the other hand, does Sergei really want to have this dysfunctional family as in-laws?

Humping the Fiancé

Vera and Sergei are in bed at the hostel. This is the notorious sex scene. Why did it offend so many Soviet viewers? First, because it was the first audacious depiction of the sex act in Soviet cinema. Even under *perestroika* a year after the appearance of *Little Vera*, attitudes to sex were puritanical. The well-known presenter Vladimir Pozner hosted *Telemost*, a live exchange between two studio audiences, one in the Soviet Union, the other in the USA. In answer to a question about sexual attitudes, a Soviet woman exclaimed categorically: 'We don't have sex!' Second, because the sex act depicted the woman on top of the man. Many Soviet women over thirty-five considered this abnormal and expressed their disgust in letters to the press.

We need to take a broader view of the scene. First, it lasts a mere 1 minute and 20 seconds out of the film's 129 minutes. Second, and more important, the significance of this scene lies less in its sexual

12. The sex scene.

explicitness and more in the light it throws on Vera and Sergei's behaviour. Yes, Vera does straddle Sergei but, at the same time as humping him, she conducts a post-mortem on his behaviour at lunch with her family. Is it any wonder that he has to adjust his penis twice, the first time during the initial interrogation and the second time, just after he is back on course, when she casually informs him that she had told them that she was pregnant. It is important to note that he does not reply to her query about whether he wants a child. He is certainly relieved that she is not actually pregnant. What sort of a relationship do they really have? Our doubts increase. Has sex become just something to do, like getting drunk, to relieve the boredom?

Prenuptial Arrangements

Events begin to snowball. The next logical step for Vera and Sergei is to visit the Register Office. Before that, however, the director wants to create the impression that Vera and Sergei are trapped. A series of intermittent, high-pitched, eerie notes accompanies a lingering shot of the harbour. We hear sirens, hooters, the lapping of the waves, and watch the sun as it fades from the smog-filled sky against the factory chimneys and cranes. Then the camera pans out towards the open sea. The open sea ought to suggest new horizons, but that suggestion is undercut by the ominous atmosphere, created by the perennial smog and heightened further by synthesised music. In fact, the smog conjures up the idea of difficulty with breathing, both literally and figuratively. In a sense, their lives are being taken over.

The Register Office confirms this. A youngish, expressionless female registrar tells them the date and time of their wedding and of the obligation to arrive ten minutes early. Just as Sergei, ever the male chauvinist, tells Vera to write down the details, the registrar interrupts, informing them that it is not necessary since an invitation will automatically be sent to them. The sheer cold impersonality of the procedure is stunning, a chilling reminder of the state 'taking care' of its citizens. There is no mention of happiness. Even the location of the bridal shop – on Metallurgists' Avenue – indicates the insularity of the town where everything is associated with its industries.

Fond Farewells at the Airport?

The camera moves from the control tower to Vera's mother, who seems to be looking out for someone. Rejoining her husband and son, she busies herself with her USSR bag during an exchange between the father and son about the financial aspects of Vera's wedding. His worries notwithstanding, the father tells him that he will breed rabbits in the winter and make hats for sale in the market. Goodbyes are said. Viktor seems embarrassed. Father tells him to bring the family next time. Through the window Mother shouts that he must send a photo of Misha. His father suddenly realises that he has forgotten the melon Mother has packed and insists on handing it over despite protests from Viktor and the check-in girl.

This scene is full of telling details: the USSR plastic bag, a sign of Brezhnev's drive towards consumerism, but inside it is an old-fashioned string bag, an '*avoska*', a 'perhaps bag'. People used to carry them around just in case they spotted anything for sale. Note Viktor's briefcase, a sign of upward mobility, at least in his eyes.

13. Airport farewells.

Note, too, the officiousness of the check-in girl. We also witness the father's conservatism. He feels it his duty to pay for the wedding. His resourcefulness is typically Russian – there is always a way to find solutions to problems, in this case a sideline in fur hats. Mother is still obsessed with food, this time with fruit for Misha. She manages to kiss Viktor twice instead of the more customary three times. 'All good things come in threes' or 'God loves the Trinity', as they say in Russian. However, it does not worry Viktor who cannot wait to get away. 'I don't want it [the fruit]. I've had enough for God's sake!' he yells in irritation. He does not even look back at the pathetic tableau – Mother and Father at the window. His treatment of his parents, bordering on rudeness, is unjustified and the viewer cannot but feel sympathy for them. They really miss their grandson and want the best for him. The window acts as a physical and emotional barrier.

Winding up the Prospective Father-in-law

Sergei has to share his room at the hostel with some African students, which puts a damper on his sex life. It is, however, Vera's decision for Sergei to move in with her. Sergei seems rather nonplussed by the decision. Does it dawn on him that this will be another step towards becoming trapped with the in-laws from hell? Although Sergei has gone along with the idea, we feel that his heart is not really in it. When they arrive at the flat, it is without enthusiasm that he mentions 'the start of a [N]ew [L]ife'. It is a cynical use of the expression which referred to embarking on a life based on communist principles. Furthermore, their room is right next to the parents' bedroom. It is hardly an agreeable prospect. Having distractedly pulled down the hanging lampshade, he turns to examine himself in the mirror. What a display of narcissism! The usual ritual of moving into a new flat is subverted when Vera wishes 'to christen' the moving-in with sex. *Her* passion is not in doubt. He simply obliges.

Reality soon sets in with a vengeance, for we next see Sergei, Vera and her father sitting, not in the dining room but round the kitchen table, the usual focal point of family life. The mother is at work. The meal consists of just bread and soup, and of course home-made vodka for Father. He wants to take charge of the wedding arrangements. He has his list of necessities. Look how Sergei baits him.

> *Sergei*: And a car with a doll?
> *Father*: Like everyone else.
> *Sergei*: And a veil?
> *Father*: We'll buy one.
> *Sergei* (grins): Veils are for virgins.

Vera tries to diffuse the situation by explaining that Sergei is only joking. Father's conservatism again surfaces with the wedding preparations. He is, after all, the father of the bride. Family pride is at stake; he does not want to lose face in front of the neighbours, insisting on giving as good a send-off as they did for Viktor and Sonia. Sergei, however, has to interject a sarcastic remark about his drinking: 'You can have a good do without us!' Once again Vera tries to smooth things over, this time by refilling Father's glass. She is just as guilty of collusion as her mother; they both complain about his drinking but do little to stop it. After the father has left, offended, Vera tells Sergei not to lay it on so thick. Sergei's response is ominous: 'He'll get used to it!' It is clear that he has enormous power over Vera. He kisses her. She responds immediately and passionately. She is hooked.

To the Future Housewife

Mother knocks timidly on the door of Vera and Sergei's room. Her embarrassment at seeing them in bed together is palpable. Her conversation is phatic. Even when she sits down, she continues to avert her gaze, merely complaining about the state of the room. She is prudish, like her husband. She gives Vera a two-volume edition of *The Homemaker*. The fact that the book is a gift from a work colleague, Inna Sergeevna, is important. Female work friends play an important role as support. Inna is the same age as the mother and probably shares the same values. The books are old and dog-eared, but still useful, but they are a sign of the generation gap. The dedication, 'To the future housewife', highly amuses Vera and Sergei, whose value system is very different.

Unhealthy Prying

A bleak shoreline. Discarded, rusted boilers, twisted rails running out to sea and a left-over lump of reinforced concrete serving as a fishing spot add to the sense of abandonment. The lapping waves suggest recurrence. Nothing changes or ever will. Sergei and Vera lie on the sand in a little cove. He reads aloud from *The Homemaker* about the importance of etiquette in creating a good impression and in forming friendships.

This is ironic in view of his dreadful behaviour at the family dinner and of the fact that he now physically hurts Vera to extract further information about her first love. This violent streak is really a power trip. The 'exchange' is in fact one-sided. Vera does not interrogate him about his past. Note also Vera's earlier ironic answer to his question about her goal in life: 'We all have a goal, Seriozha, the same one – communism.' This brought the house down in Soviet cinemas. Vera, Sergei and friends are part of 'the lost generation', those who have lost faith in communist ideals. Finally, Tolik, whom we had seen getting a tattoo at the beginning of the scene, ends it

14. On the beach.

15. Sergei hurts Vera.

with a song, the lyrics of which border on the banal. And yet it fits in with Vera and Sergei's long embrace as the waves roll in – Hollywood's *From Here to Eternity*, Soviet style.

Plutonically Speaking!

The kitchen. The mother's stereotypical function: food preparation. Note that Vera does not help. She seems to have made an effort with her dress, probably for Sergei's benefit, by adding a waistband. The mother's reported conversation with Sergei about her husband's excessive drinking reveals a classic example of collusion. She persuades herself that he will still drink, even if she stops preparing snacks. Vera does not react at all. She, too, colludes. At this stage her parents are unaware that she is not pregnant. The father returns with some shopping. This is the only time that we see him making a contribution to the running of the house, though he does not put the groceries away; that is women's work. Note that his reference to 'lover boy' is a further example of the tension caused by Sergei's having moved in. Vera says that he is still reading. The 'still reading' is like a red rag to a bull and his indolence provokes both parents to reveal their value system: ritualised courtship; a platonic relationship; hard work and a responsible attitude to money. Vera starts kissing Sergei. Just look at her mother's reaction! She slams the door. Sergei's reference to her parents as 'thick' is justified: her father had used the word 'plutonic'. Vera's observation that they are the only parents that she has is heart-breaking. Sergei is bored out of his mind, for he has nothing in common with them. Yet Vera is happy and finds it funny when Sergei asks her where his razor is, just like her father. We, however, wonder, albeit briefly, whether Vera and Sergei might become another version of her parents.

Impasse

For the first and only time we see where Chistiakova lives with her mother and half-brother, Maximka, the result, we suspect, of a liaison with a black student from the local institute. A Soviet audience might well pick up on an oblique cinematic allusion, a reference to *Circus* [Tsirk, 1936] which promoted the ideal of ethnic equality under Stalinism. Chistiakova's mother is left to bring up the child on her

16. Chistiakova and Vera in the kitchen.

17. Vera sobbing at the table.

own. The kitchen has a homely quality about it. Chistiakova and Vera are not dolled-up, they wear no make-up. They drink ordinary beer ladled out of an enamel bowl. Vera wonders whether Sergei will like her wedding dress which Chistiakova is busy sewing. Her concern is genuine, yet it reveals that, for all her bravado, she has a traditional attitude. Women must please men. Chistiakova seems to have botched the dress, but she suggests adding a bit of lace. This is an example of 'make-do-and-mend', the lot of many Soviet citizens.

Cut to Chistiakova and Vera, drunk at the kitchen table. Tongues are loosened. Vera's eyes fill with tears as she contemplates married life plagued by the constant bickering between her parents and Sergei. And what sort of marriage will Chistiakova have? For all her flamboyance she is content to settle for second best, an older divorcé, polite, placid but with old-fashioned ideas about the role of women.

Cut to Vera as she watches a funeral procession from the window. She begins to sob. This little scene is significant, sociologically and psychologically. Many deaths occur in such industrial towns, the majority through respiratory diseases. Vera's mother is asthmatic. Vera has her whole life before her, yet the funeral procession reminds her that death comes to us all. What will she have achieved? An

Analysis

insecure life with Sergei, arguments with her parents, perhaps a child, chores, and, if Chistiakova moves away, no close, female friend. Funtime is over. Reality hits home.

From Sparring to Stabbing

It is Vera's father's birthday. Against his better judgement Vera persuades Sergei to join in the celebrations: 'Just a little drop and everyone will be happy!' If only that were true. In the dining room (special occasion), Sergei and Father eyeball one another. The taunting begins. Mother tries to intervene, to no avail. Father's motto is 'Never trust a man who doesn't drink'. His remark, 'Drinking with friends is not a crime', is ironic in that he does not have any. He is an alcoholic loner.

Sergei loses his temper and drags him into the bathroom, locking him in. In his drunken state the father manages to smash the wash basin. Sergei is not a drinker but he has been pushed to the limit and now feels the need for a drink to calm himself down. Father's other example of homespun wisdom, 'A man should be boss in his own

18. Sergei loses his temper.

home', reveals his patriarchal attitudes. For him it is an unwritten law. It never crosses his mind that he might need to earn respect. When he is locked in the bathroom, full of child-like self-pity, he calls out to Vera for help, not to his wife. Once released, he and Sergei continue to trade insults until he lashes out at Sergei with a carving knife. The mother is clear who the guilty party is. 'You've killed him, Kolia!' she yells.

The Pressure Tactics Begin

A view of the skyline at dawn, accompanied by a string version of 'Vera's theme', might suggest a new beginning, but the same old cranes and smog are there.

Vera returns home from the hospital. Cut to her pitiful, vulnerable face as she lies in bed. She has taken to her bed because reality is too painful. Her mother looks on, wanting her to acknowledge that Sergei is at fault, having constantly treated her husband with contempt. This time a friend at work has given her a book about the law for Vera. She paints an awful picture of what life would be like without her husband. Vera simply pulls the covers over her head. Viktor, who has been recalled from Moscow, admits, with a semi-grin, that Vera will not listen to him any more; she is no longer his little sister. This half-grin reveals a callous streak. It is as if to say, Vera has made her bed, she can lie on it. When he prescribes tranquillisers for her, it is a purely clinical solution. There is no attempt on his or his mother's part to appreciate Vera's suffering or its causes. It is just a treatment of the symptoms.

Picnic at Wreck Beach

Under normal circumstances a picnic is an opportunity for a family to spend time together. Yet this scene reveals Vera's increasing alienation. Even the setting presages this: a deserted strand, two lonely tufts of sea grass barely sprouting from the dunes. As the family alights from the cab, Viktor helps his mother, but Vera is left to get down by herself. However, we realise that Vera does not want to be part of the company. She angrily kicks off her flip-flops, grasps her head as if it might explode, and almost throws herself down on to the sand, her head between her hands. Her father watches her, not knowing what to do. When she goes on to adopt the foetal position, her mother and Viktor discuss her as if she were not there. Vera's faded white dress reminds us of a hospital gown, as if she were a patient. It is unsurprising, then, that Viktor should put on his bedside manner, pointing to the recuperative powers of the sea and fresh air. Vera feels forced to assert her existence. She lashes out at the pretence, the family lie, the good father taking good care of the good family. Importantly, they do not even turn round to face her. Mother remains obsessed by food. Viktor stuffs his face in his selfish way. Father just stares ahead. Vera accuses her mother of duplicity over the stabbing. At least Viktor realises the gravity of the mother's course of action.

Mother's next comment is crucial: 'By the time I've finished, they won't know what's true and what isn't.' Surely this is a fair description of the family as a whole, as becomes clear in the subsequent references to the circumstances surrounding Vera's conception. Her mother did not want her (true); her father wanted a girl (untrue). Viktor is left to tell the whole truth: another child would be a ticket to a bigger flat. The father tries to intervene. He is a decent man when sober. Vera is stunned by the revelation. She pulls away to execute a yoga posture which, as Chistiakova has explained, is a useful way to 'purge yourself of all toxins and contact with external influences'. This process is a fitting description of what poor Vera is trying to do. Hers is a poisonous family. Yet her attempt fails. Vera in close-up yells, 'Shut up!' She is reduced to sobs. Mother resorts to well-worn phrases: 'Don't speak to your mother like that!' Father awkwardly seeks refuge in a swim. Viktor dives in as if the previous exchange had never taken place.

Once the rain starts, the mother reverts to type: housework tasks, gathering up the picnic things. Note that she shouts after her husband. Only later does she call out for Vera, almost as an afterthought. She is more worried about the picnic things, about the food being spoiled and about her sandals. Viktor tells her not to worry, as Vera will not catch cold. That, surely, is the least of Vera's concerns.

Cut to the cab. Viktor fails, or refuses, to acknowledge how desperate her plight is. Unconcerned, he even bursts into song. The father wonders where 'our little parasite' has got to. Even though the word is offensive, he has in the past used far worse to describe his

19. Father consoles Vera after the picnic.

daughter. The mother is preoccupied with her bag. For her objects seem to be more important than human beings. Viktor, still unconcerned, tells an anecdote.

In torrential rain the father eventually seeks out his daughter, finding her in a makeshift shelter, a rusted boat hulk, an eloquent metaphor for abandonment. They huddle there together. The father–daughter relationship thus depicted is touching. However, in the bigger picture, their family life is just an empty shell.

The Untruth, the Whole Untruth and Nothing but the Untruth

Mother has persuaded Vera to change her statement in favour of her father. She accompanies her to the police station to ensure that she complies. This is another example of the mother's narrow, clichéd view of the world: in this case, 'blood is thicker than water'. Yet, at the beginning of the film, she, as a law-abiding citizen, had insisted that Vera go to the police over the dollars episode. With Tolik's appearance some humour is injected. A parallel may be drawn between the celebrated Agricultural Show episode in Flaubert's *Madame*

Bovary, the humour of which derives from the juxtaposition of exchanges between Rodolphe and Emma with extracts from the chairman's speech in the background. Here we have Vera's interrogation side by side with Tolik's. They are both lying. Tolik, however, is used to twisting the truth, but he looks across, astonished, when Vera tells the investigator that her father does not drink very often. The effect on Vera of changing her story is apparent in close-ups and afterwards in the foyer with her mother. She actually calls her 'an old bag!' Mother's 'waste-not-want-not' attitude is revealed when she takes the tranquilliser that Vera has refused. In the street she says that she will cook a nice meal for Vera when they get home. Food, not love or understanding.

Alone

Vera visits Sergei at the hospital. She brings him apples and some broth, prepared by her mother, of course. Note that none of the patients pays any attention to the radio news. News is not real; it is just propaganda. The camera picks out the goods train as it clanks along. Its journey is as monotonous as the news. Vera wants to know when Sergei will be discharged and whether he will move back in with them. He does not know. He tells her that he has told the police that he remembers nothing. Vera begs him to forgive them. 'What for?' he asks. Vera tries to explain that they could not manage without her father.

Cut to the clanking goods train again. The noise seems to irritate Sergei, for this is when he raises his voice to tell Vera to tell her mother not to visit any more. Without asking for an explanation, Vera immediately assumes her mother's role with her query about what she should bring for him next time. When she assures him of her love, his outburst is devastating. He dismisses her. Perhaps subconsciously he is refusing to face reality: a future with Vera's parents, even if the court case is satisfactorily resolved.

Respect!

A gang of youths has gathered in the play area near Andriusha's block. One has commandeered the children's swing. They should not

52 Little Vera

20. The attempted rape.

be there. On the other hand, where else can these potential Toliks hang out in this God-forsaken hole? Vera feels vulnerable after her visit to the hospital. At first she is pleased to meet Andriusha.

However, the ensuing attempted rape is disgraceful. It shows them both in their true colours. If Andriusha is the spoilt, privileged brat, used to getting his own way, Vera reveals that she has self-respect. She 'defends her honour', symbolically at least. After all, she is engaged and in any case she decides whom she sleeps with. She spits out Andriusha, just as she had spat out the tranquilliser her mother had tried to force her to take. Her search for her earrings is psychological: she needs them, they are part of her personality; they help her to hold on to her identity.

Blotting out Reality for Good!

Vera can take no more. The mother, unaware of the attempted rape, suggests that she should marry steady Andriusha when he graduates. That is the last straw. Mother is simply incapable of understanding. She has sorted out her pickling, now she sorts out Vera's future, to her own satisfaction, of course. She conveniently forgets that Vera and Sergei's wedding is still scheduled for the next day. She proposes a drink, a rare occurrence! Father has left a little in the bottle, by mistake, one imagines. Her mother still has to have a jibe at him: he has not mended the wash basin. Vera takes the tranquillisers from her bag. Once her mother has gone to bed, Vera suddenly begins to sob violently. Eventually she takes the tablets, washing them down with vodka.

The tension is increased by a cut to Sergei in hospital, where he sits on the edge of the bed, as if wrestling with a decision.

Cut to an extremely drunk Vera. She reverts to a child-like state. Note the glee with which she lights the sparkler. Her grasp on reality is loosening. Yet, when she swallows the tablets, she uses her father's drinking expression, 'Forward, singing!' The pop song in the background is an ironic accompaniment to her activities. It is called 'It's So Good!'

Another cut to Sergei. He has reached screaming point. For him the continued hooting of the train is the last straw. It is interesting that, although both Vera and Sergei reach breaking point, only Vera

21. Vera with photograph and sparklers.

tries to commit suicide. This time the goods train may have a more personalised meaning for Sergei. It may represent the monotony, the blandness of his future life. Such an idea may well be in his subconscious, and he is not prepared to admit its truth, for when he meets up with Viktor on the railway tracks, he does not indicate that the wedding plans will have to be changed. They return to the flat together where they discover Vera lying on the floor, clutching the sparkler, a photo of herself as a child across her chest.

Endings?

This series of scenes, among the most poignant in the film, draws the strands together. Vera's attempted suicide is a last resort. She has become so alienated from society, from her family, from friends and, more importantly, from her fiancé. Viktor, once he realises what has happened, acts swiftly, which is to his credit. Vera's plea to Sergei – 'Why don't you love me, Seriozha? You know how much I love you!' – reveals the crucial difference between them. In Russian she uses a verb which suggests both capacity and depth. His love for her has been shallow. As Viktor manhandles his screaming sister out into the kitchen, Sergei remains stock-still, his head resting on the door-jamb, his eyes tightly closed. Note that both Viktor and Sergei put her photo back in the cabinet. However, whereas it is a mechanical reaction for Viktor, Sergei actually puts it back in its original position, as if to emphasise Vera's one-time innocence.

Bleary-eyed Father appears and is quickly ordered out of the way. He goes to sit in the kitchen with Sergei. Viktor's outburst, 'God, I hate you. I hate you all!', reveals the extent of his acquired bourgeois values. He resents having been born a provincial. They all remind him too much of it. The mother, woken by the racket, immediately becomes the housewife, starting to clear up the mess. No one answers her questions about what has happened and she does not insist on finding out. Note Viktor's reiteration of the phrase, 'Everything's fine'. In Russian 'Everything's *normal*!' This is ironic, given the present circumstances. The mother even uses the phrase later when she naively imagines that the family is together again and all is right with the world. She continues in housewife mode. In spite of everything she still has to pack some fruit preserves for her grandson. Viktor

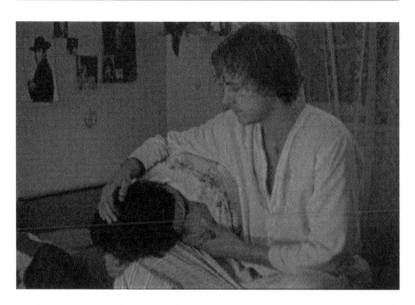

22. Final scene on the sofa-bed.

insists that he does not want the package. It reminds him of his ties. He just wants to escape, his duty done. Father irritates Viktor by asking if Vera has tried to poison herself. He then wallows in self-pity, yet unrealistically claims that he'll be taken on as a driver in prison. Viktor's parting shot is to demand that they sort things out so that there will be no court case. Father has a heart attack. We do feel some sympathy for him. After all, he dies alone, though it is ironic that he should die in the kitchen, the Soviet site *par excellence* of family togetherness. He calls out for Viktor, then Vera, but not for his wife.

Sergei joins Vera in their room. He flicks down the lampshade, just as he had done when he had first moved in at 'the start of a new life'. He tells Vera that he came back because he got scared. He, too, has experienced his share of alienation. Yet when Vera asks him whether he loves her, he does not reply.

The framing device – the panoramic view of the town – returns. Full circle. There is fine rain. A new dawn. Is there a glimmer of hope for Vera and Sergei's relationship? We shall return to this question in our discussion of themes.

3. Themes

I. This Life

'I know this life. I am not a stranger from America, or a man from Mars. I have put into this movie what I have seen with my own eyes, and reflected about. Everybody knows this life; they recognise it in my film.'[1]

Over many decades the Soviet Union fabricated an ideal image, life as it should be, rather than life as it is. The Party and its activists exaggerated, and the media obediently reported successes in industry, agriculture, construction and education. Failures did not exist. Even the arts were exhorted to toe the line. Socialist Realism, the officially sanctioned method of depicting life in the arts, required positive heroes who, imbued with the spirit of the Party, would march towards the Bright Future, thus serving as examples of model conduct for the rank and file workers. Set against this official life was the unofficial life. The term '*byt*' best describes this unofficial life. The novelist Trifonov suggested that *byt* explains 'how husbands and wives get on together, and parents and children, and close and distant relations – that too ... And the interrelationships of friends and people at work, love, quarrels, jealousy, envy – all this, too, is *byt*. This is what life consists of! We are all enmeshed in *byt* in our own network of everyday concerns.'[2]

Byt is enacted in discrete spaces, in places of work, in educational establishments, in state institutions, in the home, and in places of recreation. In theory there existed model institutions, model workers, model students, model officials, model husbands, model wives, model children and model behaviour. However, the concept of the Potemkin village (façade) was as relevant in the Soviet Union as it had been under Catherine the Great.

The town depicted in the film is Mariupol in the Donets province, Ukraine, close to the Sea of Azov. Zaporozhian Cossacks founded a stronghold at the mouth of the river Kalmius in the sixteenth century. This settlement, known as Pavlovsk in the eighteenth century, was renamed Mariupol, the Town of Mary Mother of God, by Crimean Greek settlers in 1779. It bore the name Zhdanov between 1948 and 1989. Andrei Zhdanov, who was born in the town, rose to become the Party's chief ideologue under Stalin. Profoundly anti-Western, Zhdanov helped create the myth of the superiority of all things Soviet, an idealised view of the sciences, the arts, linguistics, philosophy, technology, agriculture and education. The town serves as a major port for

---

Spaces

Macro-level (official/state)
- Industry: metallurgical, steel, coke; port, shipyards, river
- Transport: airport; buses, trams and trolleybuses
- Education: schools, PTUs, the Metallurgical Institute
- Civil and municipal: the militia (police); hospitals; the register office; housing

Macro-level (leisure)
- Parks, beach; open-air discos, cafés

Micro-level (Vera's world)
- Vera's parents' flat: kitchen, hall, bedroom, living room, balcony; Vera's room
- Andriusha's parents' flat: living room, kitchen-cum-breakfast room; Andriusha's room; stairwell
- Sergei's room in the hostel > Vera's room
- Chistiakova's mother's flat: yard, kitchen, garden

Micro-level (Vera's leisure spaces)
- Open-air disco; café; docks; beach, cove

the Donets coal basin and as a railway and road junction. Steel, machinery and grain are also exported. Almost half the population are employed in industry, the Avozstal' steel factories, chemical-coke works, machinery and metal-processing plants and fish canneries, though fish stocks have declined as a result of pollution. That Mariupol was named in honour of Zhdanov is thus not without irony. If the town could *boast* of many high schools, specialised schools, PTUs (trade schools), a Metallurgical Institute, dozens of hospitals and sanatoria, libraries, clubs and palaces of culture, cinemas, a theatre and a museum, and its status as a seaside resort, then in theory Vera should have all sorts of amenities at her disposal. Alas, there is a credibility gap. Let us now spend a moment examining this illusion–reality principle, beginning at the macro-level.

Spaces at the macro-level: official/state

Industry The Soviet Union was highly centralised. From Moscow, Stalin had imposed a command economy on the country. Through Gosplan, the state planning committee, Five-Year Plans, the first laid down in 1928, set production targets in an attempt to accelerate industrial processes in all spheres: industry, agriculture, construction and the arts. It was a highly bureaucratic system. Fulfilling the plan was the sacred duty of each and every citizen. Through the plan the Soviet Union was supposed, in theory, to outstrip the West. In practice, the plan led to unrealistic demands, massaged production figures, shoddy goods and inefficiency, yet officially it was always fulfilled.

In 1987 Gorbachev severely criticised the command economy. Though he was willing to grant relative autonomy to captains of industry, he was not prepared to abandon centralised planning. In *Little Vera* the banner over the bridge which reads 'Acceleration of Technological Progress' would not have impressed passengers on overcrowded buses. We can hear 'success' reports in the background on radio and television. Yet no one actually listens to them. Increasingly unrealistic targets had been introduced without heed of the environmental effects. Remember the panoramic views of the town with smoke belching from the factory chimney stacks and the reddish haze that hangs over the road to the airport. The smoking stacks may well have been a potent symbol of Soviet power and industrial success, but that symbol concealed a harsher reality. The history of Mariupol after its destruction by the Germans in the Second World War is deceptive. Rebuilding began in 1945. The port was later mechanised to cater for the increased turnover in the shipping of coal, ore, grain and metals. All this suggests an image of shining progress. Yet what do we see in the film? Empty fishing vessels, empty cargo boats, rusted hulks, dilapidated grain silos, a run-down infrastructure, and freight trains transporting rusted iron pipes.

Transport The standard forms of transport are available in the town: buses, trolleybuses and trams. There is also an airport and a train terminus. In the film, however, we perceive the unvarnished reality. Through the father's cab window we see a tram speeding past a chemical plant as he drives to the airport. On the return journey we see a jam-packed tram. At the crossroads, when Vera and her mother return from the hospital, an empty red and yellow trolleybus passes by. There are few cars. Given the time of day and the locations, one is tempted to conclude that the transport is basically work transport. However, it is obvious that it has seen better days. The airport is functional with just a tower and a tiny terminal building. The only evidence of originality is the propeller inserted into the fence as decoration. We notice the expressionless passengers queueing up outside. We are appalled at the peremptory tone used to give out flight information over the loudspeaker. With her 'more-than-my-job's-worth' attitude, the check-in clerk yells at Vera's father, 'Only passengers are allowed in!', reminding him of the notice to that effect on the door. The passengers surge forward with their bags and baggage. Lip-service, it seems, is applied to weight restrictions. Air travel is a necessity in such a vast country but there seems little joy in the experience. Airports are normally places for greetings and fond farewells. Not so in the film. Vera is forced to accompany her father to meet Viktor. She fails to turn up to see him off when he returns to Moscow the first time. Both this time and at the end of the film, Viktor cannot wait to escape.

Education Education in the Soviet Union was centrally planned with an emphasis on the political and moral upbringing of the Soviet citizen. Of paramount importance was the orientation of policy to the needs of the collective. 'The Moral Code of the Builders of Communism' instilled devotion to the common cause. It stressed, *inter alia*, a love of the socialist motherland and of other socialist countries; conscientious labour for the good of society; a high sense of public duty; proper human relations and mutual respect between individuals; honesty and truthfulness, moral purity, modesty in social and private life; mutual respect within the family; an uncompromising attitude to injustice, parasitism, dishonesty, careerism and money-grubbing; friendship and brotherhood among all peoples of the USSR, and intolerance of national and racial hatred; an uncompromising attitude to enemies of communism, peace and the freedom of nations; and fraternal solidarity with working-class people of all countries and with all peoples.[3] Youth organisations, such as the Pioneers (from the age of ten to thirteen) and the Young Communist League (fourteen to twenty-eight) also played a significant role in the moral and political education of young people. From the age of eighteen individuals could join the Communist Party, provided that the necessary recommendations were obtained. To be fair, we should not underestimate the overall achievements of the Soviet education system, especially the high level of literacy and the system of mass comprehensive education.

Although education underwent enormous reforms in the late 1980s, it was too late for Vera. Even so, that such reforms were thought necessary points to dissatisfaction with the system as it stood. Vera and her friends would have just completed the general educational school. At the beginning of the film she is waiting for a letter of admission to the local PTU where, after the summer break, she is to learn to be a telephonist. The PTUs were a case in point. One scholar has observed: 'The standard of such institutes was notoriously low, and they developed a reputation as a dumping ground for the least able and least disciplined students.'[4] Another commented that the PTUs 'carry the stigma of rejection or even of punishment'.[5] Vera's parents may well value education but Vera's heart is not in it. When asked by Sergei why she wants to become a telephonist, she replies that at weekly school visits to the telephone exchange she realised that 'Everyone wants to be friends with a telephonist – they think they'll get through quicker'. Hardly a well-thought-out career plan.

Sergei is a less than assiduous student at the Metallurgical Institute, though we suspect that his well-off parents pulled strings to get him in. The institute is the only place of higher education in the town. Although it may be reasonably prestigious from a regional point of view, its functional student hall of residence certainly leaves much to be desired. A twenty-four-hour concierge system still operates. The stepladder abandoned in the corridor on Sergei's floor reminds us that repairs to the roof are being carried out. The bedsteads are regulation iron ones. There is even a drop-down bed. A cupboard acts as a screen-cum-wardrobe. Furniture as such is minimal. Paint is peeling off the walls, which are painted in regulation colours. Newspapers substitute for curtains on the windows near Sergei's bed. The window-frames are rotten. There are no floor coverings. Is it any wonder that Sergei has tried to individualise the room? Cigarette packets, some of them foreign, decorate the back of the door. A sign stolen from a train depot hangs on one wall and his emblem, the cardboard tiger, stands in front of the screen.

Civil and municipal
THE MILITIA (police force) is still under the jurisdiction of the Ministry of Internal Affairs. It carries out ordinary police duties, investigation, crime prevention and the maintenance of public order. The police are poorly paid, poorly trained and poorly equipped.

They appear twice in the film. The first time they patrol the open-air disco and become involved in restoring public order after the gang fight. The second time investigators take statements from Vera and Tolik. The presence of the police at the disco seems at first sight to be too high profile for the event itself. The few girls sitting around in small groups on the perimeter of the dance floor and Vera and Andriusha engaged in desultory conversation hardly merit the three policemen with Alsatian dogs in the foreground and a further four, dog-less police sitting on a bench to the right. That two of the dog-handlers should begin to patrol seems like overkill. It is only later when the brawl takes place that we understand. Fights between gangs of youths from different districts would appear to be a regular occurrence. There is unfinished business between Tolik and members of the other gang. These gangs, in the film all-male, may well engage in brawls because there is nothing else to do in the town. On the other hand, there may well be a connection with the criminal sub-culture. After all, Tolik and Chika engage in currency speculation. What is important to note is the speed of the police intervention; it is heavy-handed and indiscriminate. Why should Andriusha be dragged off by the hair and shoved into the police van? Why should Vera be singled out, too? The over-reaction of the majority of officers, combined with the almost sadistic delight of a minority, is certainly a damning indictment.

The second time we encounter the law is at the police station after the stabbing incident. There is only one policeman on duty behind the counter. Another one walks past the mother and enters the door in the centre. The contrast between the number of officers at the disco and here is stark. The fact that the interrogation room is shared by two investigators points to a lack of office space, though sharing was also a way of making it harder for officers to take bribes. The conduct of the two investigators is matter-of-fact, though the interviews with Vera and Tolik reveal a lack of sympathy. Tolik's investigator just goes through the motions. It is as if she has already made up her mind about the sort of character sitting before her. Consider their exchange, once the first formalities about date of birth and education have been addressed.

> *Investigator*: Have you got a job?
> *Tolik*: I'm waiting for my call-up papers.
> *Investigator*: What sort of job is that?
> *Tolik*: I am not working at the moment.
> *Investigator*: So, you're out boozing.

It is as if she cannot wait to cite article 206 of the Criminal Code.

Vera's investigator is little better. He takes a glass of juice to the female investigator, yet he does not offer Vera anything, even though she has been coughing nervously. He is irritated that Tolik interrupts the interrogation to ask Vera a question. Towards the end of the interrogation he begins to have doubts about Vera changing her testimony but does not try to get to the bottom of it. He almost sighs: 'So, we'll write it down as you say it happened.'

Authenticity is achieved through everyday details. There are regulation desks and typewriters. A poster-size calendar of Nikita Mikhalkov, the famous film actor and director, adorns the wall. A bust of Lenin sits on top of the filing cabinet. There is a small aquarium, an electric fan and a drinks-fridge. However, attention is drawn to a red and gold commemorative pennant. Such a pennant would be awarded to the police for good service. This is not without irony, if we recall the level of service provided by the officers at the disco and by the investigators in this scene.

HOSPITALS AND HEALTH   The Soviet Union operated a centrally planned national health service that was, in theory, exemplary. The whole population had the right to free medical care. In spite of dedicated doctors, it was largely a façade. Staff were poorly paid; there were the inevitable shortages, especially of prescription drugs and equipment, queues were long, working spaces cramped. Relatives often brought in food for their loved ones. In addition, certain groups were privileged, especially the Party elite. From the mid-1960s to the early 1980s mortality rates worsened and life expectancy declined. For men it was sixty. Ukraine, where the film is set, was and still is below the national average. Air quality, given the concentration of heavy industry, was poor. Funeral processions like the one Vera witnesses were common. Waiting lists for sanatoria run by the large industrial plant polluters would be oversubscribed. Chronic alcoholism put additional strain on health-care services: 65–67 per cent of Soviet alcoholics drink excessively before they are twenty. Three-quarters, including girls, learn to drink as early as thirteen or fourteen. The incidence of children with birth defects being born to alcoholic mothers is high. 'In dealing with alcoholism ... the tendency is to look to the doctor, rather than to the sociologist or psychologist, on the assumption that what makes an alcoholic is the fact of drinking.'[6]

In the film we see inside the local hospital twice. A male doctor Vera approaches to inquire after Sergei's condition is in a hurry and rudely dismisses her. 'Girl, I've told you twenty times already, no one is allowed to visit him. You're wasting your time following me around.' So much for caring and sharing. Once the doctor has gone, a nurse answers her query, no doubt taking pity on her. Later we accompany Vera on two visits to the ward. The ward itself is depressing. Standard beds, chairs and bedside tables, little attempt to brighten up the area, apart from the flowers brought in by the relatives. The patients are bored or depressed. One reads a newspaper, another, who seems disoriented, is intent on handing round dried smelts from a paper bag, an accompaniment to beer drinking – we note the empty bottles on the window-sill during the second visit. A solitary chessboard lies on the sill, the game abandoned. The one-channel radio receiver seems to be the only form of contact with the outside world, and, from the news items we have heard before, it is not worth listening to. We note the total absence of nursing staff. Yet the slogan on the wall exhorts all, somewhat optimistically, 'to preserve life'.

THE REGISTER OFFICE   Marriage was also regulated by the state. The procedure for getting married was that the couple, who should be eighteen, should first apply to the local register office, the Department of Civil Registration, as it was called, where a date for the wedding would be set. The three-month waiting period was usually shortened in the case of pregnancy. On the specified date the wedding ceremony would take place either at the register office or at one of the special wedding palaces. Vera and Sergei only get as far as the application stage. We are struck by how impersonal the procedure is. The woman official is severely dressed in a black suit, her hair in a tight bun, reminiscent of a stern teacher, a representative of the nanny-state. That she is youngish is even more disturbing. (She reminds us of a younger version of Mildred Ratched, the domineering nurse from Milos Forman's 1975 film *One Flew Over the Cuckoo's Nest*.) The imparting of facts about the so-called happy day is numbingly alienating.

HOUSING   To appreciate the scale of the housing problem it is worth pointing out that during the Second World War one-sixth of the country's urban housing stock was destroyed. House-building programmes under Khrushchev and Brezhnev went some considerable way towards rectifying the situation. In the period 1956–60, the figure for housing construction was 474.1 million square metres; in 1961–65 it was 490.6; 1966–70: 518.5; 1971–75: 544.8; 1976–80: 527.3; 1981–85: 552.2.[7] While these figures are impressive, we have to bear in mind that the multi-storey blocks of flats were often built in haste in order to fulfil quotas and their quality left much to be desired. Central planning dictated a minimum floor space: 9 square metres per person. Actual conditions often fell short of this requirement. In addition, enormous numbers of people remained on waiting lists while the privileged classes jumped the queue. In the film the panoramic shots of the town show the various working-class districts with five- to nine-storey blocks. The exteriors of the buildings where Vera's and Andriusha's parents live are in need of repair. Outside there is a communal yard with a pathetic little swing for children.

Spaces at the macro-level: leisure

Parks, beach; open-air discos, cafés Parks and squares in Zhdanov/Mariupol occupy 8,059 hectares, that is, about half the total area of the town.[8] Allowing for possible changes over the past few years, the proportion is still considerable, but such figures do not take into account the state of the parks and squares. In the film the only park which seems well tended is the one which has the statue of Zhdanov with its flowerbeds and a series of flags. The panoramic shots reveal some greenery but it is shrouded in smog. Clumps of greenery can be found outside the block where Vera lives. However, as we see at the beginning of the film, these trees merely act as a frame for a huge chimney billowing smoke in the background. The railway track is overgrown with grass and weeds. Just as the factories invade the landscape and pollute it, so, too, the goods train invades and pollutes the children's little play area.

Elsewhere there is a piece of land with trees in the background and a hoarding to honour municipal leaders. Beyond that is a sculpture representing a plane soaring skywards. Yet on this piece of land, in front of the board of honour, Tolik gets into a brawl and one of his attackers throws a flare-gun in the direction of the sculpture. In theory it is one's civic duty to respect land, property and officials. In practice it is different. When Vera returns for the last time from the hospital, she crosses a stretch of land towards the railway track. It looks like common ground, yet logs have been set on fire there. The camera pans back to reveal a gang of kids sitting on a fence nearby, bored out of their minds. It is probably they who have caused the fire. One of the boys sits on a child's swing.

There are a couple of beaches; one resembles a wasteland, with abandoned, reinforced concrete blocks. The other is a proper sandy beach, where the family have their ill-fated picnic. The beach is otherwise deserted. There seems to be only one open-air disco for the area. With its wooden benches, perimeter hoarding and its stage lit by fairy lights, it certainly fails to inspire. The café we see in the film is also typical of the pre-*perestroika* period: nondescript Muzak is provided, Soviet style, by a tape-recorder standing on the counter. There are a few tables and chairs and a few equally nondescript pictures on the walls. Few customers frequent the place. There is one waitress, who appears only when summoned. There is a reminder, displayed prominently on the counter, to the effect that something is forbidden. It is hard to read but it probably refers to a ban on the consumption of non-café food.

All of this is the macro-level. We are dealing with the presence of state or official facilities. Much more significant, however, are the absences. There is no reference to youth organisations, to palaces of culture (community centres for recreation and self-improvement), or to cinemas. Ignored are the theatre (Mariupol has a drama theatre) and the museums (there is a local history museum and a museum in honour of Zhdanov). Libraries are not mentioned (there are twenty-six). The town council and the Party do not feature, apart from the board of honour already mentioned. The point is that Vera and her friends have been alienated by the system, as can be seen by their cynical attitude to official rhetoric. Here are some examples:

> *Sergei*: Do you have any special goal in life?
> *Vera*: Of course I do! We all share a common goal, Seriozha, and that is communism!
> *Sergei*: Who was that bitch I got off with? Is she a friend of yours?
> *Vera*: Yes, we're like sisters!
> *Sergei* (with a smirk): 'R-i-g-h-t ... we are all brothers and sisters!

Tolik, having downed a bottle of beer in one, declares: 'Ah, my Pioneer childhood!'

Vera, amused that Viktor wants to phone their mother after discovering Vera's relationship with Sergei, laughs: 'Don't do that. It'll put the kibosh on this month's production targets!'

Chistiakova, seeing that Sergei is smitten with Vera, remarks: 'Oh, this is the birth of a Bright, New, Soviet feeling!'

Sergei, moving in with Vera, sighs: 'Ah, a New Life is beginning!'

These macro-level spaces stand in sharp contrast to the micro-level spaces, to what I call Vera's world. It is significant that there is no word in Russian for 'privacy'. This may be explained by the fact that, officially, the needs and wishes of the collective should take precedence. Personal space is a relative term.

Spaces at the micro-level: Vera's world
Let us look now at the physical characteristics of this world.

Vera's parents' flat This is a typical, two-bedroom flat. It is self-contained, consisting of an entrance, a hall, a bathroom and a toilet off a narrow passage, which leads to the kitchen. Off the hall is the dining room-cum-living room, which can also double as a spare bedroom. It leads to a balcony. At the end of the hall, next to her parents' bedroom, is Vera's room. The rooms are primarily functional, though a few personal touches have been added, like the black and white wall hanging and 'sunflower' lights. As has been mentioned, the cramped conditions of the flat are emphasised by the way in which the hand-held camera tries to avoid bumping into the characters. Authenticity is created through everyday detail. In the kitchen, for instance, we see a standard fridge, a grimy cooker, a tiny sink, a small, wooden table with a plastic tablecloth, simple, wooden chairs, drab, two-toned walls. The windows are double-glazed (to retain heat in the winter) with a small, hinged pane for ventilation purposes (to relieve the heat in the summer). There is a functional clock and an old-fashioned single-channel radio receiver. The table is usually cluttered with pots and pans, dishes, bottles of beer, food or the father's makeshift storage jars, like the used Beefeater gin bottle. There are space-saving devices like the wall-hooks for cooking utensils, the small shelf for containers and the hanging, metal drainer. The kitchen, which is predominantly the mother's domain, is witness to the constant cycles of food preparation, serving and consumption. Like most Soviet families, this family usually eats in the kitchen.

The bathroom and toilet off the kitchen are tiny. We know that the light needs mending; the wash basin, too, which the father smashed in a drunken stupor. The interior of the parents' bedroom is seen only once when Vera has to put her drunken father to bed. Again the details are authentic: a bed with separate, red-quilted duvets and an alarm clock on the bedside table. This is the only specifically designated bedroom.

The dining room-cum-living room is used for special occasions such as Viktor's 'home-coming' meal, the lunch in honour of Sergei or the father's birthday. We see the usual parquet floor, protected by a multi-coloured rug, standard mahogany, add-on units or co-ordinated cabinets, matching table and chairs. A silver-plated fruit bowl stands on the table. A small sofa-bed is also glimpsed there when Viktor comes to stay, for space is at a premium. In order to individualise the room a little more, family photos, ornaments, glassware and a pennant are on display in the units. The family can afford only a few units, which explains the expanse of wall to the right, bare except for a long, narrow painting. A lone, indoor, potted plant is to be seen on top of one of the units and a hanging decorates the side. There are wall-lights and a central chandelier-type light. A shiny cassette deck, a sign of consumerism under Brezhnev, is displayed in one of the units. Note the absence of books.

The balcony is used for drying clothes. The bamboo curtain, which acts as a screen between the balcony and the dining room, has seen better days. The absence of plants may be due to pollution problems or to the fact that they would be another chore for Vera or her mother.

Vera's room serves two functions: a bedroom (a sofa-bed takes up much of the available space) and a room in which to relax. Vera has individualised the room with her posters of film and pop stars, her childhood doll, curtains matching the colour of the sofa-bed covers, lace curtains and a vanity mirror behind the door.

These accumulated details serve to anchor the family in a clearly defined working-class reality.

However, certain spaces in the flat acquire other meanings. The kitchen features significantly eight times. It is the focal point for the whole family, the first room members enter when they come home. Here they can unwind, eat, drink and talk. It is, or should be, a shared space. Yet it appears as a site of conflict at the very beginning of the film. The mother and father row about Vera's behaviour. In the scene where Vera clears up after her drunken father and tries to get him to eat, it is a site of reinforced conditioning. The parent–child relationship is reversed. The kitchen again becomes a site of confrontation, between the father and Vera in Viktor's presence, when she is subjected to but ignores her father's drunken, personal insults, and later between the father and Sergei. Their argument over wedding plans leads to a mutual trading of insults, with Vera as an unsuccessful mediator. The kitchen's traditional function sometimes does not last long. For instance, after the mother has told Vera of her conversation with Sergei about the father's drinking, it degenerates into a site of confrontation when the father returns. Mother joins in the criticism of Vera and Sergei. After the visit to the police station, the kitchen becomes a site of non-communication. No one listens. No one understands Vera's feelings. Just before the attempted suicide, the kitchen becomes a site of non-comprehension. Mother assures Vera that her future lies with nice, comfortably-off Andriusha. Vera, staggered by such a view, starts on her potentially lethal cocktail. In the finale, the father dies in the kitchen, calling for his son and daughter, not his wife. The kitchen is thus the site of the death of family life as such.

The dining room is normally a shared space for joyful family get-togethers. Yet, at one stage it is invaded, so to speak, by the father who commandeers the cassette deck to combine listening to Vysotsky's songs and drinking himself into a maudlin state. In the 'home-coming' scene the room takes on other meanings. It begins traditionally as a place for a family dinner. However, Viktor's pontifications about family life, endorsed by the parents, reveal the falsity of such attitudes. Here the room becomes a site of double standards. From then on the dining room appears as a site of confrontation. The specially prepared lunch, arranged so that Vera's parents may meet Sergei, is a disaster. Finally it becomes a site of despair with Vera's attempted suicide.

The balcony figures four times. At the beginning of the film Vera stands there alone eating cherries. Here it represents an escape from the mother and father's rowing over her behaviour. In the opening sequences, this personal space is invaded by her father on two occasions, so that it becomes a site of conflict and confrontation. It is on the balcony that Vera later confides to her mother that she is pregnant. She wants her to tell her father. The balcony in this instance is a site of attempted reconciliation, a sort of neutral zone. The final scene on the balcony involves Viktor and his mother discussing the need to prescribe tranquillisers for Vera. The balcony in this case becomes a site of collusion, through which Vera's independent existence is denied.

The importance of Vera's room is made clear the first time we see it. A long panning shot reveals the posters from right to left and back again. Vera is being highlighted as a young individual, a normal young girl interested in the usual paraphernalia of adolescence. Vera has escaped from her parents' arguing. It is, however, not a total escape, since the door is left open and Vera watches her mother as she telephones Viktor in Moscow. Her mother has her back turned. Later Vera again escapes to her room to avoid her drunken father, yet he invades that privacy to talk about Viktor and Sonia. Vera leaves. Although she escapes to her room to avoid her father's name-calling, after it has been discovered that she has slept with Sergei, her father still follows her, hammering on the door. She flinches visibly but the door is securely locked. When she and Sergei move in, the room, in the absence of her parents, immediately becomes a site of passion. Yet the camera makes it clear just how close the parents' bedroom is to Vera's. The adjustment will not be easy, especially for the parents. This is illustrated by the mother's subsequent embarrassment at speaking to Sergei and Vera as they lie in bed. Subtle changes have taken place: Sergei's sexy pin-up poster adorns the wall. The room becomes a site of routine, shared domesticity. Remember Sergei asking her where his razor is. Vera still loves him at this stage. Once Sergei is in hospital, the room becomes a site of attempted control. Vera's mother wants her to change her statement about the stabbing. Lastly, Vera, after her rejection by Sergei and her suicide attempt, lies on her sofa-bed in the foetal position. Eventually joined by Sergei, she asks him whether he loves her. Silence. Vera's room has finally become a site of ambiguity.

Other spaces The other spaces in Vera's world become progressively closed off to her. Sergei was originally the sole occupant of the room at the hostel. That room no longer functions as a site of sexual activity when foreign students move in at the end of the summer vacation.

Vera and her friends had been able to relax at Andriusha's parents' flat. That well-appointed flat (breakfast bar, superior quality wall units, shelves full of books, elegant coffee cups, ceramics, decorations, goldfish bowl, state-of-the-art music centre, video with foreign tapes, and separate bedrooms) is contrasted with Vera's parents' flat. At the farewell party Andriusha's mother tries to persuade Vera of the advantages of a match with her son. Vera makes it clear to Andriusha that she is not interested in him. After Andriusha's attempted rape in the stairwell towards the end of the film, there is no more contact with Andriusha and his family.

Vera also visits Chistiakova who lives in her mother's somewhat run-down house, out of town. It is a more relaxed place. This is perhaps the mother's influence. We see the result of her relationship with a student happily running around in the yard, watering the garden or watching cartoons on television. Chistiakova's kitchen is a site of friendship, of intimacy, of support. We note that it is Chistiakova, not Vera's mother, who makes Vera's wedding dress. That site of friendship will become closed off when Chistiakova goes away with Mikhail Petrovich.

Spaces at the the micro-level: Vera's leisure spaces
Once she has met Sergei, Vera abandons the disco and the café. She no longer goes to the docks. However, she does go to the beach. This is the space occupied by slag heaps and slabs of reinforced concrete. The area affords some privacy. Tolik, for instance, gets himself tattooed there, away from prying eyes, from officials. It is the 'alternative' beach, so to speak, for the younger set. Vera and Sergei find a secluded cove. It is quite romantic. Their bodies are entwined; but all is not what it seems. This is the scene where Sergei interrogates Vera about her first lover. Sergei inflicts pain on her. Sergei's use of physical force stands in contrast to the romantic setting. Even though they embrace afterwards, the viewer remains uneasy about Sergei. They do not visit the cove again. The beach has become a site of ambiguity. Vera is taken to the proper beach by her parents and brother. The beach, they think, will be good for Vera, who is depressed after the stabbing incident. Yet this beach turns from a site of health and recuperation to a site of conflict and alienation. Vera learns that her parents only conceived her to get a bigger flat. However, there is a partial resolution of the conflict at the end of the picnic, when her father tries to comfort her as they huddle together in the rain under a rusted ship's hulk.

So, all these sites I have mentioned play a role in the progressive alienation of Vera. Whereas official spaces have little value, personal spaces become ever more ineffective. Vera's last space – her room, at first an adolescent's room, then briefly a shared room – becomes at the end of the film the site of an unpredictable future.

II. Progressive Alienation – the Cold Summer of '83

Let us now examine relationships and the interactions between characters in the film. These relationships are to be found in two major areas, in families and in friendships. Several complex bundles of relationships may be compared and contrasted.

Relationships within the family

Let us first place the Soviet family as an institution within a historical framework. A radical overhaul of the relationship between men and women was undertaken in 1917. The first domestic relations code (1918) established the principle that husband and wife were mutually responsible for supporting each other in cases of incapacity and for maintaining and educating their children; they were also permitted separate property.[9] Women could decide on their own married names and were no longer obliged to follow their husbands if they changed jobs and moved. A husband could even take his wife's name. Only civil marriages were recognised. Alexandra Kollontai's maternity insurance scheme provided for eight weeks' fully paid maternity leave, free pre- and post-natal care and cash allowances.[10] The distinction between legitimate and illegitimate children was abolished. Divorce could be obtained immediately by mutual consent. A decree of November 1920 legalised abortion. In 1927 equality was granted to de facto marriages. The divorce process itself underwent further simplification and gave rise to the so-called postcard divorces, whereby if only one of the partners wanted to end the marriage and the other failed to turn up at the register office, the latter was notified by a printed form.[11]

By the 1930s Stalin had become absolute ruler. The bourgeois family having been abolished, the time to create the Soviet family had arrived. Stalin's measures were incorporated into the 1936 Constitution. Divorce regulations and rules governing alimony payments were tightened up. Family bonuses were made available. Child-care and pre-school networks were expanded. This was the new official image of the family, one that emphasised stability and productivity. Further changes were incorporated into the edicts of 1944: wives who produced large families were awarded heroines of motherhood medals and bonuses. Abortion was no longer automatic. Unmarried, childless men were to be taxed. Although de facto marriages ceased to be recognised, motherhood bonuses and additional bonuses for nursery/kindergarten places, holidays and sanatorium treatment were extended to unmarried mothers and 'productive' women.[12] Two years after Stalin's death abortion on demand was restored. During Brezhnev's era of stagnation (1964–82), divorce proceedings were simplified.

Although the material situation of most families improved, life for them was humdrum, as *Little Vera* illustrates. Most Soviet housewives faced the so-called double burden; indeed, the problem still remains today. In theory, the Revolution had given women equality with men. In practice, things were different. Most married women had two jobs, one in the workplace, the other in the home. After an exhausting shift at the factory, she would have to do the shopping, cook dinner and do all the other household chores before going to bed. Soviet researchers calculated that housewives spent about 150 billion hours per year on housework-related activities. In one survey, conducted in an industrial city in the late 1960s, two-thirds of the women interviewed complained about their lack of time. According to a 1985 survey, women spent more than twenty-eight hours a week on domestic chores. On a working day women had on average 2.24 hours of free time (data for manual and non-manual workers).[13] And what about the role of the husband in the home? Very few working-class husbands in this patriarchal society would help with the running of the household. Those who did would spend ten hours per week, according to the 1985 survey mentioned above. On a working day men had on average 4.03 hours of free time. Soviet men preferred instead to watch TV or read the paper, more often than not with a drink in their hand.

This last point is crucial for an understanding of *Little Vera*. Consumption of alcohol in the Soviet Union doubled between 1960 and 1980. Home-brew (*'samogon')* was enormously popular. Alcohol abuse was frequently cited in divorce cases. Although various anti-drink campaigns had been launched, actual anti-alcohol policies were relatively mild because alcohol made such a significant contribution to state finances through taxes. Soviet research programmes concentrated on the medical effects of alcohol abuse rather than on the social causes of the disease.[14]

Vera's family Kolia (the father) is a driver, Rita (the mother) a production quality controller in a local factory. They were born in the late 1930s. In many respects they are simple working-class people with clearly defined gender roles. Their value system and their social patterns of thinking have been fixed by their upbringing. They both set great store by education, at whatever level, medical or call-operator training or even general knowledge. 'When we were your age, your mother and I were already working,' Kolia informs Vera, and continues: 'We've worked our fingers to the bone to give you and Viktor a good start in life.' Their philosophy is of the commonplace, traditional variety: '"Look after your honour from your youth up",' says Kolia, alluding to the well-known maxim. 'Don't talk to your brother like that, he's older than you,' Rita admonishes Vera. 'There's lots of vitamins in bread!' she advises the family gathering. She relies on popularising reference books like *The Homemaker* and *The Legal Handbook*. Kolia is angry that Vera did not ask their permission to get married. 'I wish I'd listened to *my* mother before I got married,' Rita tells her daughter. Morals aren't what they used to be, she acknowledges with a sneer: 'With you lot it's just hello and then the repercussions!' 'What will the neighbours say?' is one of Kolia's frequent, tell-tale remarks. Even though he dislikes his future son-in-law, his conservatism makes him all too conscious of his obligations as head of the family: 'You'd better send a telegram to Mongolia to let your parents know about the wedding. My brother and I can lend them the money […] Viktor got a proper do and so will you!' In spite of their difficulties both the husband and wife muddle through. Even though Kolia's stop-gap schemes for breeding rabbits for fur hats or growing melons will probably never materialise, no one can deny that he and Rita both work very hard. Alas, he drinks too much, with disastrous consequences. Rita resigns herself to it. They row, bicker, yell and shout, but they hardly communicate with one another in any real sense of the word.

Viktor's family In his father's eyes, Viktor has made something of himself by becoming a doctor. Yet we feel that he has used his education in order to leave behind his working-class background and enter the white-collar sector. He rarely brings his wife and son to visit his parents. In fact, he reluctantly admits to Vera and Kolia that his marriage is on the rocks. Deep down he is petty bourgeois and hypocritical. He is a purveyor of double standards as regards family and marriage.

Sergei's and Andriusha's families These families have a different social standing from Vera's and both are materialistic.

We learn little about Sergei's family, except that his parents are away working in Socialist Mongolia and will not be back until the following year. In Mongolia they would have access to privileged shopping facilities. They can certainly afford to send Sergei money for his designer clothes. They are probably not without connections in that they have managed to sub-let their flat, which explains why Sergei finds himself initially living in the student hostel.

Andriusha's background is naval. His father is probably a merchant fleet officer whose wife does not need to work. Their flat is tastefully decorated. Given his job, the father would have access to privileged shops as well as the opportunity to visit foreign ports, which explains many of the expensive items in the flat, his wife's elegant kaftan and her expensive ring and bracelet. She has the time and the money to take care of herself. This contrasts strongly with Vera's mother. Yet, at the same time, she shares Rita's conservatism. For instance, she uncritically accepts her wifely duty, meeting her husband when his ship comes home after its six-month absences. If Vera and Andriusha get married, she will expect Vera to join her in this ritual.

Lena Chistiakova's family Lena's mother's life has been unorthodox. We recall Lena's remark in the café: 'If my mum had got married each time, I'd have four dads.' The absent father, or, to put it another way, the single mother, was common in the Soviet Union. Lena's mother had become pregnant by a black man. Significantly she had decided against abortion. Some of her mother's nonconformity has rubbed off on Lena.

None of these families is a model family. To some extent they are all dysfunctional, failing to live up to the image of the ideal Soviet family, an image that the state had created and had striven to promulgate. These are the real Soviet families.

Let us now examine the relationships within Vera's family in more detail.

Father and mother

> They fuck you up, your mum and dad.
> They may not mean to, but they do.
> They fill you with the faults they had
> And add some extra, just for you.[15]

It is striking how few exchanges there are between the father and the mother. Many of them reveal the tension in the relationship. Their voices are usually raised. Rita's very first words take the form of a reproach shouted in Kolia's direction from the kitchen. Distressed by Vera's conduct, she yells: 'Just look at her! She's left school but God knows what they filled her head with. It's all your fault. You spoiled her when she was young!' Kolia manages to ignore her to begin with. After the first altercation with Vera, he returns to the kitchen and demands his food. It is interesting that this first interaction also establishes the gender roles: the mother as giver, the provider of food, the father as the receiver, the consumer of food. Both have obsessions, she with food, he with home-brew.

Rita seems to have her feet on the ground. It is she, not her husband, who telephones Moscow to get Viktor to come home and

23. Mother's hands.

sort out the situation with Vera. Kolia does not object to this. In this he is weak. We may assume that it is again Rita who asks Viktor to return after the stabbing incident. She feels her husband does not do enough around the house. The bathroom light remains unfixed.

The first time we see Rita acknowledging her husband's fondness for the bottle and the distress it can occasion is when she returns home after a shift to discover that Viktor will be arriving in a couple of days' time. Yet she is more concerned about whether her husband has eaten or not. She wearily tells him to keep his voice down. And this is one of the few occasions on which she actually addresses him as Kolia; usually he is addressed as Dad. Here she takes on the role of the mediator. She is used to his antics. When he seems to have an attack, she merely ignores him, even stepping over him as he lies on the floor. 'Here we go again!' she sighs and simply goes about her business in the kitchen. She is used to holding her own. 'Your daughter's a slut!' is met with, 'She's yours, too!' Disliking bad language, however, she does not repeat the offensive word. Before the lunch in Sergei's honour, she tells her husband not to swear. She has a simple code of behaviour. 'It's not nice', is an expression she frequently utters.

Rita tries to learn from others: from Sergei the importance of savouring a wine's bouquet, for instance, though her husband's reaction is merely to sneer at such pretension. In any case, wine is for women, vodka is for real men. She cannot see what other people can see. She fails to acknowledge that she is colluding with her husband over his drinking. She defers to her husband in matters of education and status, for example, by merely endorsing her husband's use of the word 'plutonic' and warning Vera: 'Your father won't let you get married!'

In spite of the frequent rows, this unambitious pair actually need each other. 'They're the only ones I've got,' Vera remarks. Similarly, Kolia is all Rita has and vice versa. They are loyal to one another. Rita is even prepared to insist on Vera perjuring herself over the stabbing to protect her husband. Almost at the end of the film she remarks: 'We're all fine [in Russian 'normal'], we're all together again.' In one sense, the couple does revert to 'normality', that is, to what they understand as normality. Kolia sits at the kitchen table to have another smoke, Rita wipes the table, scolds her husband and withdraws. A few minutes later, Kolia suffers a heart attack. He does not call out for his wife. The relationship is truly over. In the film their marriage has been depicted, warts and all. She is no model wife, he no model husband.

Father and son; mother and son   The relationship between father and son is to some extent conventional. Kolia is proud of Viktor for having 'made something of himself'. Viktor has accepted his father's belief in the value of education. They share some of the same attitudes. Neither is seen helping in the kitchen, though Kolia does once bring home the shopping. Viktor does not offer to help fix the bathroom light. They take their place at table merely to be served by the womenfolk. Never once does Viktor talk about his own family in any normal sense. Father and son also share a love of alcohol, though the son is not an alcoholic. He is seen drunk only once in the film, when he calls on Sergei at the hostel. There is, however, little affection shown between the two. At the picnic on the beach, despite the tension, they go off for a swim. Like father, like son; it is as if neither wants to face reality. Yet there is a bond between them. As Kolia experiences the fatal heart attack at the end of the film, he calls out for Viktor.

The relationship between mother and son is special. He was her first-born and for her he subconsciously replaces her husband in terms of reliable support. Between them they agree Vera's treatment, a prescription for tranquillisers. On the other hand, Rita treats him in the same way as she treats her husband: he is there to be fed, be it fruit compôte, bread and soup, a banquet, or stocks of preserved vegetables and a melon to be shared with his family in Moscow. Even Kolia acknowledges this trait. When he tells Rita that Viktor will be visiting, he yells: 'You'll have to start baking!' Viktor resents his mother's insistence on his taking the fruit back to Moscow because it forms a link between him and his provincial family. Viktor is there to be chided, like her husband. 'Vitya, behave yourself!' she exclaims at the lunch for Sergei.

Viktor, as we have already noted, avoids reality, yet he insists others should face it. His final outburst sums up his feelings for his parents: 'Sort it out so that there's no court case [...] My God, I hate you all!' The problem is that neither of them understands what he means.

Mother and daughter; father and daughter Vera's relationship with her mother is quite hostile. As we have already noted, it is from her mother's lips that we hear the first words of criticism. She continues: 'She'll be the death of me! [...] She loafs about all over the place [...] She won't listen to us!' The use of 'she' indicates the distance between them. The first words Rita actually addresses to Vera are accompanied by banging on the bathroom door. Vera has locked herself in. Rita shouts her name – 'Verka' – a form often used for naughty children, but Vera is eighteen years old. A peremptory 'Come here!' is her mother's final outburst in the opening scene. She expects Vera to put her drunken husband to bed.

Rita sends confusing signals. When Vera tells her that she wants her baby to be a boy, she calls her a fool; girls are useful around the house. Yet she has to scold Vera twice for not washing the floor. Nor does she send a positive message about marriage: 'Don't get married, get yourself an education [...] What do you know about love? I loved your father when I got married and had to take on him and his three brothers and the allotment. No one lifted a finger to help me. That's where love got me!' She lacks empathy when it is most called for, bluntly telling Vera how she constantly suffered from morning sickness while she was carrying her. She demands that Vera perjure herself over the stabbing incident to save Kolia. Yet at the same time she becomes angry with Vera for lying about her pregnancy. There is one rule for Rita, another for other people. The worst part, however, is the revelation that Vera had been 'an accident'. Instead of having her aborted, they kept her in order to get a bigger flat. Even after Vera has run off from the picnic, having heard this, Rita does not seem unduly worried. 'She'll come back by herself.' At no time does she try to comfort Vera by showing her real affection. Her solutions are practical: make broth for Sergei; shove tranquillisers down Vera's throat. The last straw is when she suggests that Vera should marry Andriusha. A nice life and money, too. She fails to understand that Vera has attempted suicide. All she can think of is packing some preserved fruit for Viktor to take home to Misha. Sustenance for the body, not for the soul. Not once does she inquire after Vera. Tomorrow she will sweep the mess up, figuratively shoving everything under the carpet. All will be well with the world. Everything will be fine, back to 'normal', so to speak.

The relationship between father and daughter is much more complex. There is a strong and special bond between them, as is evidenced by the scene after the picnic scandal. Kolia dashes off in the driving rain and hail in search of Vera. He shouts her name: 'Vera! Vera! Verka!' Note again the form used for naughty children. He finds her huddled, shivering, under the keel of a rusted, abandoned boat. The camera then observes father and daughter in close-up. She rests her head on his shoulder. He has his arms round her. He tenderly pats her back and nuzzles her hair. It is a very powerful and emotional moment, intensified by the music, 'Vera's theme', and by the fact that no words are exchanged, or at least cannot be heard. His lips move slightly, we can only guess that he is uttering a simple consoling phrase.

Yet, in the rest of the film we have seen a different side to the father's character, which clouds the issue. In many societies it is common for there to be a strong father–daughter bond. How often do we hear expressions such as 'Daddy's girl' or 'my little princess'? Freud wrote about the Elektra complex, according to which the daughter feels a subconscious attachment to the father, and at the same time antagonism towards the mother. The daughter eventually overcomes this attachment and, through marriage, enters into a relationship with another man. However, as Horton and Brashinsky have astutely observed: 'Vera is unable to negotiate her emotional and psychological life between her father and Sergei. If her father had been a traditional Russian patriarch, the separation would have been easier.'[16]

What image, then, does Vera build up of her father in the course of the film? What signals does she receive from him? Kolia is authoritarian in his attitudes as his observations confirm. When Vera informs him that Viktor had told her to respect her parents, he agrees with the sentiment. 'A man should be the boss in his own family!' he declaims at his birthday party. He thinks it right to play the heavy-handed father. In the opening sequences of the film, for instance, we note the following remarks addressed to Vera, who, of course, ignores them. 'Am I talking to myself?' 'Damn it, I'm talking to you!' Later, after Viktor's lecture on family relationships, which Vera knows is hypocritical, he yells: 'That's typical of you. Instead of listening …' So far as he is concerned, certain rituals have to be followed, including wedding arrangements. He has his pride. Everything must be done properly, otherwise he will lose face in front of the neighbours. Education is the ticket to a better life, better than his and Rita's.

It is, however, when he is drunk that Kolia reveals that he is less than a model father, especially where his daughter is concerned. Here are some of his revealing outbursts:'You slut! We didn't thrash you enough when you were a child'; 'You dockside whore!'; 'As for getting married, and without asking your parents' permission, I'll beat this nonsense out of you!' he screams as he hammers on Vera's door. It is a case of impotent rage. The marriage will take place in any case. He even insists on playing his part in the preparations.

Vera's attitude to her father's drinking is a mixture of concern and resignation. She tells him quite openly that he drinks too much, that it is bad for him. Yet she advises him merely to cut down. She is even fond of his special drinking phrase 'Forward, Singing!' At the lunch for Sergei, she completes the second part for him, with a laugh. Both she and her brother emulate him in their drinking habits. Viktor drinks to excess at the hostel, probably because he is away from home. Vera gets drunk after Andriusha's farewell party and at Chistiakova's, though on the latter occasion it is to drown her sorrows. However, whereas Viktor's drinking is not criticised by his father, Vera's is. He attempts to smell her breath in the lorry on the way to the airport. Her reply is sharp and to the point: 'Smell your own!' Father's double standards again. There is, however, one scene where the relationship is seen in a different light. Vera comes home to find her father drunk, listening to Vysotsky. Here she is no longer the daughter, but a substitute wife and mother, and her father is the child. This is a pattern that had begun when she was younger, as he sentimentally reminds her, without the slightest comprehension of his own inadequacy. Despite the slanging matches, they do love one another, but he fails to live up to her expectations as father-hero. He cannot see that Vera's behaviour is partly his fault. He may blame others – Chistiakova, his wife, Sergei – but alcohol prevents him from facing reality. At the end of the film, tired though sober, he does ask Viktor whether Vera had tried to poison herself. Whether he understands her reasons is another matter.

Brother and sister When they were younger, he was the big brother, she the little sister. Their relationship has changed over the years. We see this from two conversations, one at the beginning of the film and one towards the end.

> *Mother* (to her husband): I'm going to telephone Viktor. Let him have a word with her. She'll listen to him.
> *Mother* (to Viktor): Make her understand. She used to listen to you.
> *Viktor* (with irritation): Yes, she used to, when she was a little girl. *He leaves.*

Vera sees through Viktor, sees him for what he is: a hypocrite. She is not taken in by his lecture advocating a negotiated family life; in fact it reduces her to raucous laughter. Earlier she had drawn her own conclusions about the real state of his marriage when Viktor revealed that he and his wife had decided to have a break from one another. When he discovers her together with Sergei at the hostel, he is outraged. Morally he is on shaky ground, however. What really annoys him is the fact that he has been caught out by Vera. As we have seen, Viktor is not averse to some extra-marital dalliance. On the other hand, knowing Sergei's reputation, he may genuinely have Vera's best interests at heart. 'He'll always have girls round his neck. He'll be bored with you in a week, max!' he shouts. Later during the special lunch at home he can hardly contain his anger. He tries to warn the family about Sergei.

After the stabbing incident Viktor is again summoned from Moscow. At the picnic, after all the shouting and yelling between Vera and Mother, it is Viktor who blurts out with brutal insensitivity the circumstances surrounding Vera's conception. How did he come by this piece of information? Presumably from his father in one of his previous drunken chats. The effect on Vera is devastating. After this incident, not once do we see Viktor comforting Vera as a brother. For example, when Vera enters the kitchen as Kolia is telling him about one of his money-making schemes, Kolia insensitively asks Vera: 'Why the long face?' She does not answer. Viktor remains silent, concentrating instead on eating. He has no idea about Vera's state of mind, he merely prescribes tranquillisers. 'They work on the base of the brain,' he declares. Brain not heart, we note. What more is needed? In fact, when he returns to collect his things before leaving for Moscow again, he sees her lying on the floor with her photo and her sparklers, and grins!

Condescendingly he says, 'Clever girl, excellent!', thinking she is just drunk. When he suddenly realises what has happened, he tries to save her. But it is as if he were dealing with a case in casualty. He follows all the right procedures. He even takes the bottle of pills away. Big brother cannot wait to leave. In effect he abandons his sister.

The importance of friendship
Russian is particularly rich in proverbial sayings about friendship.

> It is better to have one hundred friends than one hundred rubles.
> To see a friend, seven versts[17] is not out of one's way.
> Tell me who your friend is and I'll tell you who you are.
> An old friend is better than two new ones.

Living under a totalitarian regime, Soviet Russians had to choose their friends carefully. Although the political situation had improved by the beginning of the 1980s, there was still a tendency for some people to have as friends those they had known for a long time, especially from childhood. In many cases friends would play an even more important role than relatives or close family members. In moments of personal crisis, the first port of call would be a friend.[18] Vera's mother exchanges family news with Inna Sergeevna, her friend at work. Her copy of *The Homemaker* is handed on to Vera. Another workmate gives Rita a copy of a book about the law, which is also passed on to Vera.

The gang or *'tusovka'* Vera belongs to a gang of sorts which comprises her closest friend Lena Chistiakova and Andriusha and Tolik. They represent her peer group, having been at school together until the summer. Vera also knows Chika, Tolik's speculator friend, though we do not see them together. This is a group for hanging out with, for whom '*kaif*' is all-important. The word means '[h]aving it all, grooviness, or catching a buzz ... For some [it] means fashionable clothing ... [or] a videotape collection ... [or] alcohol. It means having everything and they want it now, not in some far-off Soviet utopia.'[19] It also includes sex. Vera and her friends may live in the provinces and be relatively unsophisticated, but they still want their share of the action, so to speak, even though this will inevitably lead to parental conflict, to that universal phenomenon known as the generation gap.

For Lena, Andriusha, Tolik and Vera, 'moderation' is an alien concept, especially so far as alcohol is concerned. Although Tolik hangs out with Vera, Andriusha and Lena as friends, he differs from them in one respect: he is involved in a local all-male gang. He is image-conscious and streetwise. He probably thinks he is cool, with his thin moustache, yellow vest and gaudy trousers. He is not averse to using a broken bottle in a fight. He has a tattoo on his chest to reinforce his image. He lives dangerously, getting involved in speculation with Chika. However, there is another side to him. He is cynical. Remember his comment associating his drinking habits with his Pioneer days. He is not quite as cool as he thinks. He wears a more sober T-shirt when he goes to the police station in order to create a better impression but also to hide his tattoo. His few French phrases are just for show. The song he sings as he strums his guitar on the beach is cloyingly sentimental:

> At the appointed time, the evening star rose above the rooftops.
> Like the distant pole I'm so far from you.
> But I hear your voice.

Tolik uses his friends, scrounging money from Lena for alcohol, for instance. He is actually scared of Chika – twice he asks Vera to speak to Chika about the missing dollars to get him off the hook. He lies to the investigator in Vera's presence. This scene brings home to her the gravity of her own course of action. She comes to realise that Tolik is no longer the type of friend she needs.

Individual friendships: male to male and female to female The contrast between the two sets is marked. Whereas Viktor is basically conservative, Sergei is non-conformist. Even their choice of underpants is telling, Y-fronts versus Speedos. Our first impressions of the relationship between Viktor and Sergei are formed when Viktor, drunk, barges into Sergei's room at the hostel, without realising, of course, that his sister is in bed with him. Viktor's first words immediately inform the viewer of Sergei's reputation as a stud. 'Why do all the girls fancy him?' he sings. He then remarks: 'Where is *our* tiger? Where is *this hostel's* throbbing sexual pulse?' [emphasis added]. It is as if he automatically assumes that Sergei has a woman with him. When Vera inquires who it is, Sergei replies that it is an old friend

24. The tiger.

and goes to greet him. They have obviously known each other for some time and are on intimate terms. They shake hands, embrace and use the familiar 'you'. A young woman appears in the doorway and seductively announces: 'Vitia, we're waiting for you. We're getting impatient!' So, Sergei and Viktor are two of a kind. Viktor is judged to be worse because the viewer knows that he is a married man. His marriage is admittedly shaky but Viktor is determined to make the most of this visit, without Sonia his wife. We recall that he rarely brings his wife with him, so it would be feasible to suggest that this is not the first time that he has behaved this way. Once Vera appears, his double standards show.

Viktor and Sergei are representatives of what we would call laddish culture. They can sleep around. However, when it is a question of Sergei sleeping with Viktor's little sister, that is a different matter. At the special family lunch he even tries to warn the family about Sergei but nobody listens. Towards the end of the film Viktor bumps into Sergei who has just discharged himself from hospital. His opening remark is full of sarcasm: 'So our patient has escaped. Vera *will* be pleased. When's the wedding?' No further words pass between them. If Sergei had not become involved with Vera, the friendship between

Sergei and Viktor would probably have continued. A superficial friendship with only two things in common – chasing women and refusing to grow up.

On the other hand, the female to female friendship, as exemplified by Lena Chistiakova and Vera, is much more solid, at least to begin with. Vera refuses to accept her father's opinion that Lena is a bad influence. Vera is quick to use Lena as a convenient excuse not to have to watch videos alone with Andriusha. When we see Vera and Lena together for the first time on the dance floor, the camera catches their essence immediately as it moves from their identical black shoes, to their identical black fish-net stockings, and finally to their identical, black, miniskirts. They use their gaudy tops, baubles and streaked hair to stand out from the crowd. They provocatively jiggle their bodies in unison. Vera and Lena are girls out for a good time. They are spontaneous. With Lena Vera suddenly comes to life. They may not be sisters, but they are soul sisters.

At the café it becomes clear that Lena is a romantic at heart. For her, people in love write letters to each other when separated. It transpires that she also writes her own poetry. Although she had been the first to single out Sergei at the dance and continues to throw herself at him when he appears at the café, once she realises that it is Vera he is attracted to, she is irritated but is astute enough to cut her losses. She does not bear a grudge. At Andriusha's farewell, they sit together, Lena's hand on Vera's shoulder. They are still friends. At the drunken party which follows, they again sit close together. In a quiet moment, she asks Vera how things are between her and Sergei. 'Wonderful!' Vera replies. 'Really?' Lena almost whispers, now fully resigned to the state of affairs.

Lena and Vera appear together for the final time in Lena's mother's kitchen, where Lena is finishing Vera's wedding dress. The atmosphere is tense. Lena seems sullen and irritable. Vera, too. Lena's expression remains constant throughout the scene. Gone is the carefree attitude. Vera confides in her about the relationship between Sergei and her parents. Lena tries to be supportive. After a few more drinks, Vera paints a depressing picture of life at home. Lena lets slip that her relationship with Mikhail Petrovich is also difficult. One of the unwritten rules of close female friendship has been broken: women friends should be completely open with each other. Lena has kept her prospective marriage from Vera. The repercussions will be far-reaching. Effectively, Vera will lose her friend when Lena moves away with her new husband. Another step along the path of alienation.

Suitors and lovers We must dwell a moment longer on the Lena–Mikhail Petrovich relationship, because it forms a contrast with Vera and Andriusha's and Vera and Sergei's relationships. What is Lena's view of the divorced Mikhail? She was aware of his situation right from the start. She agrees with Vera that he is old, but adds: 'He is polite and calm.' After a pause she adds: 'Always.' We recall how he brought flowers for her to the boat. He teaches her yoga. He also insists that she should not attend college after the summer break. He wants everything on his terms. Furthermore, in her alcohol-fuelled conversation with Vera, Lena does not mention the word love. In going off with the arch-conservative Mikhail Petrovich, she puts aside her romantic notions and settles for someone second-best, but at least she has someone.

Vera has always made it clear that Andriusha is just a friend. He is certainly not the man for her, as becomes evident at the disco and at his farewell party at home and on the barge and in the stairwell. She shows her superiority, vigorously defending herself as he tries to rape her. In the end, we see him for what he is – a despicable, spoilt brat.

Sergei, on the other hand, represents for Vera someone out-of-the-ordinary, someone with film-star quality. Initially the relationship is purely physical. After the disco Sergei eliminates Andriusha from the picture, then extinguishes his cigarette, takes Vera's hand, and, squeezing her jaw, exclaims: 'Come on!' Vera pushes him away. Sergei refuses to take no for an answer. Just as he takes her one and only cigarette, so he will take her. He is determined that she will be another notch on his bedpost. In the very next scene she is seen leaving his bed in the hostel. This is where the trouble starts. When she asks him whether he loves her, he hesitates before replying, 'Of course!' She wants to believe him. Later, in the café, he asks her if she loves him. 'Yes!' she exclaims, without hesitation. At the end of this scene they retire, not to the cinema, but to bed.

In Viktor's presence she claims that she and Sergei are having 'a big romance'. Sergei, probably acting on an impulse, suddenly declares that he wants to marry Vera. After Viktor has left in high dudgeon, Sergei paints a clichéd picture of marriage: waking up together each morning, the wife preparing nice meals for him. Vera accepts this gender-based notion, though she jokes about her cooking skills.

It is time for Sergei to meet the future in-laws. He appears in his totally inappropriate gear, taking delight in registering their shock. Having sized up the situation, he decides to have some fun, particularly at Vera's parents' expense. He makes it clear that he is better placed than they are. He avails himself of generous helpings of the food, fully realising that this is an opportunity not to be missed, for we recall how in his hostel room he had existed on tuna straight from the tin. He wolfs down the food, talking with his mouth full, the way Vera's parents do, and then further insults them by suddenly and rudely leaving, taking a nonplussed Vera with him.

The importance of the ensuing sex scene lies in the debasement of emotions. Not even sex for sex's sake. Gone are the tender caresses, gone are the words of love, to be replaced by carping criticisms about his behaviour over lunch, the admission to her parents of her pregnancy and denial of the same to Sergei. When Vera finally asks him whether he wants a baby, significantly, he does not answer.

Yet this ill-matched couple continue with the relationship, even going to the authorities to register their intention to wed. When they move in with Vera's parents, Sergei goes out of his way to offend her father. Vera is fully aware of this but cannot help herself. One long kiss from Sergei is all it takes for her to be won over. Even after he has shown his penchant for manipulation and his cruel streak by inflicting pain on her to extract a confession about her first love, the scene in the cove ends in a passionate embrace. Sergei's self-centredness comes more and more to the fore. He reads alone in their room. He is bored out of his mind. He expects her to know where his razor is. The bickering continues, as we have seen from her conversation with Lena, '[h]e hates them and they hate him'. At Kolia's birthday party more accusations fly: Sergei is not a real man because he does not drink; he is tied to his fiancée's apron strings; he will leave Vera. Vera tries to calm the situation down, but to no avail. As we know, the evening ends tragically.

Vera plays the dutiful fiancée and visits Sergei in hospital. On the last occasion he informs her that he does not want any more visits from her mother. When Vera tells him that she loves him, he tells her to go home.

Why does Vera attempt suicide? Spaces and people conspire against her happiness. The first factor in the equation is the environment in which she lives. The haze that hangs over the town serves as an appropriate metaphor. Created by the gaseous emissions and smoke from the steel and coke plants, the atmosphere is oppressive and stifling. All the characters are affected by it in one way or another. The town is run-down. We recall the docks, the dilapidated silos, the rusting ships, poor transport. The town offers few opportunities for leisure pursuits: the public beach, the main park, an open-air disco. The beach is empty, the park, too. The disco becomes the venue for a fight between rival gangs and the focus of police brutality. On the other hand, it is at the disco that we see different aspects of Vera's personality. Dolled up, she is alive, vibrant and out to enjoy herself. She has a sense of her own worth. As an innocent bystander, she refuses to be dragged off by the police. On that same evening she is her own woman in that she has made it clear that she does not want a relationship with Andriusha. Yet the conversation with Tolik underlines her naivety. She had allowed him to hide Chika's dollars in her handbag, and this got her into trouble at home.

The beginning of her downfall can be traced from the moment she meets Sergei. Lust at first sight on his part, love at first sight on hers. At least she finds some privacy in Sergei's room, away from the oppressive parental flat and the constant bickering. Each time there is a row at home, Vera escapes into her own room, but, given the size of the flat, her room does not afford her complete privacy. We have noted how hostile her mother appears towards her. For her father she is 'his little girl' who also, paradoxically, takes over on occasions as his wife, feeding him and putting him to bed when drunk, nagging him about his drinking and playing the role of family mediator, when necessary.

Once Sergei asks her to marry him and the so-called pregnancy is revealed, relationship patterns change. Space opportunities, too. Viktor washes his hands of the affair and returns to Moscow. When Vera has Sergei move in, their privacy is severely curtailed because their room is next to her parents' bedroom. The father–mother–daughter relationship alters. It is now father versus prospective son-in-law and vice versa, with Vera and her mother as pigs in the middle, so to speak. The relationship between Vera and Sergei suffers. After the stabbing incident, Viktor returns but can only prescribe tranquillisers. Vera finally acknowledges her mother's double standards: advice to be law-abiding and hand Chika's dollars to the police at the beginning of the film and her insistence now on perjury to save her father from jail. She has to face her parents' deceit over the motive for her conception. Sergei in hospital finally tells her to go home. Andriusha tries to rape her in the stairwell. Her mother tells her that it would be better for her to marry Andriusha. No wonder Vera is at her wits' end.

Her alienation is complete: the gap between Vera and her parents has become unbridgeable. The kitchen and dining room are now only sites for confrontation. The old gang no longer hang out together. She is about to lose her best female friend, and her kitchen-haven in the country. She has seen Andriusha in his true colours. And, last of all, Sergei has abandoned her. She cannot take any more. Suicide is the only way out.

III. Cycles. *Plus ça change. Plus c'est la même chose?*

Frames
Two panoramic shots of the city serve to frame the events of the film. The first takes us from night to morning, revealing the smog-bound city. The second begins a new day. At the same time, the action is punctuated by shots of a goods train as it clanks back and forth between the station and the industrial complex to load and unload its rusty iron pipes. We have already suggested that the train's progress and its shoddy freight represent the monotony and futility of the enterprise. The production of unwanted and substandard material in itself gives the lie to the state's production claims. However, the train's progress suggests a secondary meaning. It represents the monotony and futility of the lives of the citizens of this town in general and of Vera and her family in particular. Everyone leads, or is expected to lead, this treadmill existence. Vera's father drives his truck back and forth, back and forth. They can try to escape it, but

Themes 91

25. The goods train.

it gradually wears one down. It is no surprise that Sergei cannot stand the sound of the train towards the end of the film. He has had to listen to it day in and day out while in hospital.

At the end of the film Sergei wearily slumps down on the sofa-bed next to Vera. 'Why did you come back?' she whispers. 'Because I was afraid,' he replies. 'Do you love me?' Vera asks. There is no reply. The father dies on what should have been their wedding-day.

The ambiguous ending?
We might be tempted to speculate that Vera and Sergei will get married and that their marriage will simply mirror her parents' marriage. Let us not forget how Sergei, like her father, asked Vera where his razor was. The perpetual cycle, the fixed gender roles, the rows. Sergei, like Kolia, has no real friends. Vera has lost hers. Yet this couple will stay together because of their future children. If that does indeed come to pass, then it is a very gloomy prospect.

Another possibility is that, with her father's death, Vera will be free to start out on her own marriage. She has grown up. Two other observations are called for that support this suggestion. First, Vera's very name is important. In Russian it means 'faith'. Its significance becomes clear by the end of the film. In spite of all her troubles, of everything she has to put up with, in spite of her environment, she none the less has not lost all her faith. She has 'a little faith', so to speak. There is a glimmer of hope. A helpful biblical allusion springs to mind. 'According to your faith be it unto you' (Matthew 9: 29). Second, the final panoramic shot is different from the opening one. It is raining and the sky is much brighter. It is as if the rain has washed away the pollution, the oppressive atmosphere. A ritual cleansing is hinted at.

The credits have rolled. The lights in the cinema have come up. We are about to leave. In our mind's eye we see Vera and Sergei still sitting huddled on the sofa-bed. What are they thinking? Perhaps of Chekhov's words at the end of *The Lady with the Lapdog*: '[B]oth of them knew very well that the end was still a long, long way away and that the most complicated and difficult part was just beginning.'

Notes

1. Quoted in Hedrick Smith, *The New Russians*, New York, 1990, p. 112.
2. Iurii Trifonov, 'Net, ne o byte – o zhizni!', in *Kak slovo nashe otzovetsia*, Moscow, 1985, p. 102.
3. Paul Hollander, *Soviet and American Society*, Oxford, 1973, p. 149.
4. Lynne Attwood, *Red Women on the Silver Screen*, London, 1993, p. 111.
5. Andrew Wilson and Nina Bachkatov, *Living with Glasnost*, London, 1988, p. 56.
6. Report quoted ibid., pp. 149–50.
7. Quoted in Geoffrey Hosking, *The History of the Soviet Union* (2nd edn), London, 1990, p. 511.
8. <www.mariupol.dn.ua>.
9. Louise E. Luke, 'Marxian Women: Soviet Variants', in Ernest J. Simmons (ed.), *Through the Glass of Soviet Literature. Views of Russian Society*, New York, 1953, pp. 31–2.
10. Richard Stites, *The Women's Liberation Movement in Russia. Feminism. Nihilism. Bolshevism 1861–1930*, Princeton, NJ, 1978, p. 369.
11. Ibid., p. 386.
12. Ibid., pp. 388–90.
13. Vladimir Shlapentokh, *Love, Marriage and Friendship in the Soviet Union. Ideals and Practices*, New York, 1993, pp. 189–90. The data from the 1985 survey comes from David Lane's *Soviet Society Under Perestroika*, London, 1992, p. 259. For a depiction of the life of Soviet women in literature,

see Mary Seton-Watson, *Scenes from Soviet Life*, London, 1986, pp. 13–36.
14. Archie Brown, Michael Kaser and Gerald S. Smith (eds), *The Cambridge Encyclopedia of Russia and the Former Soviet Union*, Cambridge, 1992, pp. 464–5.
15. Philip Larkin, 'This be the Verse', *High Windows*, London, 1974.
16. Andrew Horton and Michael Brashinsky, *The Zero Hour. Glasnost and Soviet Cinema in Transition*, Princeton, NJ, 1992, p. 114.
17. An old Russian measurement: 1 verst = 1.06 km.
18. Shlapentokh, *Love, Marriage and Friendship*, p. 244.
19. Nancy Traver, *Kife. The Life and Dreams of Soviet Youth*, New York, 1990, p. 4.

4. *Little Vera* and the Soviet Youth Film

Once Lenin had identified the ideological potential of cinema in the moulding of the individual, it was clear that youth would become one of Soviet cinema's primary targets. Yet it was a slow start. Perestiani's *Little Red Devils* [Krasnye diavoliata, 1923] and Olga Preobrazhenskaia's *Fedka's Truth* [Fedkina pravda, 1926] were the first examples of the genre. A firm moral tone was stressed. The masses and youth in particular were to become the builders of communism from 1928 onwards and cinema's duty was inspire them, to create positive heroes for the millions. Even if children fell by the wayside, they could be helped to see the error of their ways. The first film to problematise the youth issue was Ekk's *Road to Life* [Putevka v zhizn', 1931]. Even in musicals of the 1930s the 'message' took precedence – anyone can succeed – from street to Soviet, from Komsomol to Komsomolsk, from *kolkhoz* to Kremlin, all with Party help and the assistance of the collective. Second World War films offered self-sacrificing patriotic heroes as role models. Relationships between the sexes were comradely and proper, as can be seen in the Vasilev brothers' *Chapaev* [1934]. During the Thaw which followed Khrushchev's destalinisation campaign in the mid-'50s, different genres, such as the war film, the urban film and the school film, addressed youth issues and gave sympathetic portraits of the characters as individuals: Kalatozov's *The Cranes are Flying* [Letiat zhuravli, 1957]; Grigori

Little Vera and the Soviet Youth Film   95

Chukhrai's *Ballad of a Soldier* [Ballada o soldate, 1959]; Tarkovsky's *Ivan's Childhood* [Ivanovo detstvo, 1962]; Raizman's *And What if This is Love* [A esli eto liubov'? 1962]; Mitta's *My Friend Kolka* [Moi drug, Kol'ka, 1961, adapted for the screen by Alexander Khmelik from his own play]; Rostotsky's *We'll Get by till Monday* [My dozhivem do ponedelnika, 1968]. The popularity of the school film continued into the 1970s with Solovev's rites of passage film *One Hundred Days after Childhood* [Sto dnei posle detstva, 1974] and Gubenko's moving *Orphans* [Podranki, 1977]. Some film-makers felt that during Brezhnev's era of stagnation the nation had lost its way morally and used the 'school' as a metaphor for society. Dinara Asanova's grittily realistic *Tough Kids* [Patsany, 1983] and Bykov's harrowing *Scarecrow* [Chuchelo, 1984] serve as excellent examples. The first film teaches us that so-called tough kids do not deserve to be written off as hopeless cases or simply ignored by parents, teachers or society at large. Who, after all, made them what they were before they were taken under the wing of Pasha Antonov, who runs the work and sports camp for delinquent waifs and strays? The second film asks the question: what price the collective?

There is, however, one particular film that paved the way for *Little Vera*. With the advent of *glasnost* and *perestroika* under Gorbachev, cinema looked into many dark corners of Soviet society. Youth was no exception. The mother of all *perestroika* youth films was made by a Latvian director, Jūris Podnieks. His documentary film was called *Is It Easy to be Young?* [Legko li byt' molodym? 1986]. Podnieks' original intention had been to interview teenagers about their hopes, dreams and anxieties and then to return to them ten years later to see how they had fared. However, a certain event took place that was to change both the idea and the scope of the film. Podnieks knew that a rock concert featuring a popular Baltic band was scheduled to take place in Ogre, near Riga, on 6 June 1985. Thinking the event might prove interesting, Podnieks took a few shots and left. A news item the next day reported that fans had vandalised the train in which they were travelling home. This incident became the background to the film. The film eventually became a mosaic, offering a bleak portrait of the 1980s generation, covering a host of youth problems. Themes and issues are manifold: the generation gap, the lost generation, alternative lifestyles, officialdom, tradition and conformity within a nanny-state, and moral malaise. These are the same issues that we find in *Little Vera*. Podnieks' film had asked: 'Is it easy to be young?' The answer was a resounding 'No!' Vera's answer is the same. If anything, it had become even harder for her. *Little Vera* was not the only film to take up the moral issues raised by Podnieks. Others were Abdrashitov and Mindadze's darkly menacing *Pliumbum or A Dangerous Game* [Pliumbum ili opasnaia igra, 1987], Shakhnazarov's gentler *The Messenger* [Kur'er, 1987], and Riazanov's disturbing *Dear Elena Sergeevna* [Dorogaia Elena Sergeevna, 1988]. The heroes and heroines of all of these films are a far cry from the model youth so beloved and promoted by the state. It was only *glasnost* that made possible the making of *Little Vera* and these other films.

5. Reception

Awards

At the Venice Film Festival in 1988 Vasili Pichul was honoured with the FIPRESSI award (International Cinema Press Federation). Also in 1988 the film won the Special Jury Prize at the Montreal World Film Festival and the Golden Hugo at the Chicago International Film Festival.

In a competition organised by *Sovetskii ekran*, in 1988 readers voted *Little Vera* into the second place, the first place going to Alexander Proshkin's *Cold Summer of 53*. The same readers voted Natalia Negoda best actress of the year. Statistics from this competition are revealing. Of the 30,054 readers who cast their votes, 24.9 per cent were between the ages of eighteen and twenty, 23.7 per cent were between twenty-one and twenty-four and 17.4 per cent were between twenty-five and thirty. Only 8 per cent were between thirty-one and forty, 4 per cent between forty-one and fifty-five and 1 per cent over fifty-five. Liudmila Zaitseva, Iuri Nazarov, Andrei Sokolov and Alexander Fomin also figured in the best actor category.[1] Zaitseva and Nazarov were further honoured at 'Constellation', the first ever All-Union Festival of Soviet Actors, which was held in Kalinin (now Tver) in 1989. This was 'for best-supporting roles' and 'for the artistic representation of social types'. Negoda was singled out for 'a role which has become an event in public life', as it was quaintly put. Pichul's wife, Maria Khmelik, won the 1989 European Film Award for best screenplay.[2]

The Viewing Public's Response

In the Soviet Union the public flocked to see the film upon its release, over 50 million people in less than a year.[3] Many viewers felt compelled to write letters about the film. A selection of letters to the editor of *Sovetskii ekran* appeared in 1989, and Maria Khmelik published a selection of letters addressed to the film's creative team as a postscript to her post-film novel which appeared the following year.[4] Here are two opposing views from *Sovetskii ekran*:

> Please pass on my letter to that wretch of a director. For the fourth day now I have been going around with a feeling of disgust and loathing. I am not a hypocrite, nor am I a prude, but there's got to be a limit. Is this what glasnost is all about? Being subjected to swear words and pornographic scenes? It's awful. You call it art? And public and taxpayers' money is being spent on this! [A.F., Voronezh]

> *Little Vera* is a complex film ... [I]t touches many a sore spot ... [R]espectable members of society are angered by it. What are the schools doing? What are parents doing? Why didn't they teach their daughter simple right and wrong? But, tell me, how can a woman bring up her daughter when, from morning till night she's at the factory and by the end of the working day she has hardly the strength to make it to her bed with her string bags full of shopping? ... How can a father bring up his daughter when he's out making long-distance trips to earn a decent wage and is at home with the family only about twice a week and when one of those days needs to be spent unwinding with a bottle before setting out on another long-haul trip? So, the girl grows up on the streets with her more street-wise girlfriends cultivating the spirit of the scrap heap and the student dorm. Yes, the film is a sharp social documentary. Problems of upbringing, the moral face of society, the problem of women at work and in the home. Who is going to answer these questions? [Saur Z., Labinsk]

Maria Khmelik's postbag, which contains letters written by people from all walks of life and all age groups, reveals similar attitudes:

> You must be Jews, because you obviously know all about the filth you show in *Little Vera*. [Anonymous, Moscow]

> We were so sickened we had to walk out halfway through. Since

[then] we have heard that the people who made it are only in their twenties, they obviously don't know who should lie on top during sexual intercourse, so they show little Vera (a prostitute) getting on top of a man (a parasite). [Seven anonymous women from Moscow who have all been married for between thirty-five and forty years]

[I]t was so realistic, it might have been going on in the landing outside my flat.
We're always being forced to watch films that tell us how things should be, and this leads to the cult of personality. We've had enough of that. Your film catches ordinary people's family life perfectly: the scruffy fridge and the tiny kitchen all give exactly the right atmosphere. It's right to show these things. And the holes in the heroine's dressing gown are a brilliant touch too, because that's what it's usually like, and we don't all wear satin dressing gowns. The language in the film is also very clear and familiar, for instance that scene with her parents, and further on you show our Soviet police very well, because people think they're heroes, when they don't do a damn thing but put on uniforms. [M.V., Moscow]

What you've shown us is the complete truth, a concentrated dose of it of course, but no worse than what happens in any 'normal' family ... I myself have grown up in a family where everything seems fine on the surface, but in fact we are all strangers. That's the tragedy of it! And they don't even want to do anything about it. [M.P., Ivanovo]

Vasili Pichul himself had been shocked by the reactions in his home-town, to which he had returned for the première of his film.

My mother said, 'You have insulted us. You have put our family's whole life up on the screen in front of the whole Soviet Union.' When my parents walked down the street, people pointed at them. One woman pointed at my mother and said, 'Is your family life really such a nightmare? Is our daughter so awful?' My mother couldn't handle it.

Hedrick Smith comments on this quotation, suggesting that 'blue-collar workers, [although aware that] their misery had been exposed in order to reform it, [actually] recoiled from change, preferring the old familiar hell'.[5]

The Critics' Response

Masses of reviews appeared in respected newspapers, in the tabloids, in film journals and on the Internet. Both Western and Soviet critics stressed the film's historical and sociological importance. The following quotations are representative:

Richard Corliss: 'In [Vera's] sharp defiant voice you can hear the sound of breaking glasnost' (*Time*, 10 April 1989, p. 72).

Philip French: 'With glasnost Russians now have the opportunity to look at themselves in the most unflattering, realistic light' (*Observer*, 11 June 1989).

Henry Sheehan: '[A] pioneering look into the grim desperation of the contemporary Russian working class' (*Hollywood Reporter*, 28 April 1989, p. 73).

Anna Kagarlitskaia: '"Aren't you ashamed to show all of this?" a woman sitting in the darkness of the hall ... at the première of *Little Vera* exclaimed angrily. "And aren't you ashamed to live like this?" a voice replied out of the same darkness. Primordial, stimulating truth' [*Ogonek*, 14 July 1988, p. 16).

Andrei Plakhov is one of the few critics to draw comparisons. *Little Vera* and Mike Leigh's *High Hopes*, which shared the FIPRESSI prize in Venice, deal with similar issues. 'For all the biting sarcasm of the treatment of the heroes, neither author considers his characters monsters. The screen is suffused with sympathy for their "little faith" and their "high hopes"' (*Sight and Sound*, no. 2 [1989], p. 83).

For Lynne Attwood, a Slavist and sociologist: '*Little Vera* turned many of the old Soviet values upside-down ... Family ... Motherhood ... Sex.'[6] Anna Lawton, also a Slavist, saw it as 'a realistic commentary on the disintegration of the social fabric'.[7]

More substantial and more far-ranging discussions of the film can be found in the pages of the major Soviet film journal *Iskusstvo kino* and in a special Soiuzinformkino collection entitled *Dumaite o reklame* [Think about publicity]. The former is a fourteen-page debate between Elena Stishova, a leading film critic, and Iuri Davydov, a philosopher and sociologist. Four topics are addressed: the environment and conscience, one-dimensional people, the tragic dimension of the film, and the riddle of Sergei's return. Basically, Stishova and Davydov are trying to assess the extent to which the environment and the absence of moral absolutes are to blame for the situation in which the characters of the film, both the older generation and the younger 'lost' generation, find themselves.[8] Stishova opens the discussion with some observations about the Soviet youth film. She is of the opinion that Dina Asanova's *Tough Guys* was the first film to show difficult children as products and victims of their environment, of specific social conditions.

Although the ensuing discussion is rather free-wheeling in a typical Russian way, some of the views are thought-provoking. For Davydov, the truth does not lie either with the older generation, or the younger generation. There is a need for an arbitrator – Truth. He thinks that characters in the film are unaware of how tragic their situation is. The earlier the adolescent accustoms him/herself to adult privileges (Vera starting to smoke at fourteen and her involvement with her physics teacher a year later), the longer the adolescent wants to remain an adolescent. Eventually s/he becomes an adult who continues to lead the life of an adolescent with no responsibilities. A stranger to moral absolutes, s/he goes off the rails (drink, sex, drugs, for instance).

For Stishova, Sergei's function is to show that there is a rung even lower than the one occupied by Vera's family. He is deeply cynical, even more than Vera's brother. There is a certain caustic irony in the fact that Pichul and Khmelik have deliberately made Viktor a doctor. Physician heal thyself!

The Souiuzinformkino collection offers articles that were specially written before a group of films went on general release.[9] One section is devoted to *Little Vera*. The editors were apprehensive that audiences might fail to appreciate the film's 'profound, moral meaning'. They wished to engage certain 'groups of people, such as educators and the parents of teenagers, who by virtue of their work or family life have most contact with adolescents and who often encounter mutual incomprehension and enmity, which sometimes leads to serious consequences'. The editors proposed to distribute extracts from this material to cinemas, local papers, film clubs, youth clubs and other educational establishments in order to provoke discussion. In a way, the articles become a sort of study guide similar to those produced by Film Education in Great Britain. However, the Soviet version tends towards the didactic. 'Following the authors of the film, viewers should see in the bitter experience of the heroes not a cause for mutual accusations but a plea for help and charity.' The editors consider that, 'for *glasnost* to become a reality ... family relationships need to be restructured, different generations need to learn to understand each other, and not to destroy but to create their own spiritual world'.

To be fair, the articles themselves are, on the whole, balanced. In a press release entitled 'Leave the wilderness', A.M. Shemiakin argues that there is a danger in regarding *Little Vera* as a *chernukha* film. To do so inevitably leads to a polarisation of attitudes – those who admire and those who oppose such an approach. Neither of the groups denies that the life depicted on the screen exists but the question is whether or not such details ought to be shown. Shemiakin feels that any attempt to paraphrase the plot is doomed to failure. Everything becomes so banal. His own attempt does reveal some valuable insights, however. For instance, he notes that the mother, as she desperately tries to keep house, 'meticulously sweeps the floor, without realizing that, figuratively speaking, the house is on fire'. For Shemiakin *Little Vera* is the portrait of the sickness in a society at a critical stage in its development. Hopes have been dashed. There are only illusions left. In the film, as with Dostoevsky, it is a question of the saving of the soul. Yet, to suggest that 'a lack of spirituality' [*bezdukhovnost*] in society is the cause of the sickness is pointless. Despite everything, Vera does still have some sort of 'faith', even though she and Sergei have no refuge other than each other. The film asks whether it is possible to salvage this 'faith' before it is too late.

In 'Faith, Hope and Love', a perceptive address to cinema clubs, Z.K. Abdullaeva argues that the life and attitudes of Soviet filmgoers have long since been coloured by a sort of social romanticism. *Little Vera* goes back to the traditions of Russian realism, exemplifying Chekhov's conception of drama according to which 'everything on the stage should be just as complicated and at the same time just as simple as in life'. The real effect of the film lies not in its sensational entertainment value but in the fact that the extreme incidents that happen to the characters are so ordinary, almost normal. The theme of the film is the survival of a person as an individual. It is surviving as an alternative to vegetating. Abdullaeva points out the difficulty of surviving in a polluted town where there is nowhere to go and nothing to do. At the same time, and this is surprising, it is easy to live there.

Vera's parents are still alive; her father loves her; her brother may have escaped but it takes just a phone call and he is back, as if still attached by the umbilical cord. Alas, nothing works out. Nobody notices the cramped conditions, the pollution, or the poor amenities. Apart from eating, drinking and sleeping, going in for yoga or tattooing, there is little else.

Abdullaeva singles out the scene at the police station for comment. The absurdity and the normality of everyday life intersect. Procedures are followed, yet for those giving their testimony or those trying to make sense of it, understanding is impossible. The scene is a metaphor for that absolute failure to understand that dogs the characters in the course of the film. Abdullaeva ends with this question: 'When a tattoo in the shape of a cross becomes a substitute for inner sufferings, when a child's photo on a chest replaces an icon, when ... parents ... hope for the best, and children, for whom all roads are open, wait for the worst to happen, where can one find the strength for the bright Future?' She concludes that the answer lies in compassion: in that very compassion with which Pichul has endowed his characters.

Although D.V. Dondurei is the editor of *Iskusstvo kino*, he trained as a sociologist. It is in this capacity that he contributes to the debate. He points out that Soviet society is experiencing a sea change; there are different priorities, different interests and different attitudes to morality. For example, he quotes the results of a survey conducted in 1986 among senior pupils in Moscow, Leningrad and Erevan and Ashkhabad. Asked to prioritise careers, they gave first, second and third places to black-marketeers, speculators and car mechanics, respectively. Diplomats came tenth and professors sixteenth, the lowest. He reports that only one in four graduates actually use their qualifications. He gives depressing statistics about the break-up of the family. The majority of couples who do remain married do not want live-in parents. Another piece of research conducted in Moscow and Tula revealed that of 300 couples under thirty, who had been married for three to four years, every tenth man and every fourth woman admitted to contemplating suicide. In the light of this he considers Vera's suicide attempt to be genuine. Dondurei also writes at length about widespread sexual ignorance and the lack of contraception. Although he admits that *Little Vera* does not address all of these problems directly, he none the less feels that 'it is an accurate representation of the reality, which has been literally woven out of these problems'. This 'socially hyper-realistic film does not judge anyone', nor does it make a statement; it just shows life as it is. Nevertheless, he hopes that people will demand change.

Still other reviewers and critics concentrated on the heroines of the film. Verina Glaessner, for instance, contends that

> it is around the character of Vera and her friend Chistiakova that the film becomes less comfortable and less predictable. To some extent, it appears a sour *hommage* to the Czech New Wave, with the two girls as depressed second cousins to Věra Chytilová's larky heroines in *Daisies*, their whimsical, though far from light-hearted, anomie providing ironic comment on the world in which they live.[10]

Marina Drozdova plays down the social aspects of the image of Vera, preferring, wrongly in my opinion, to see her as 'the very embodiment of an erogenous zone'.[11] Tatiana Moskvina, a young and independent-minded film critic from Leningrad, agrees. She celebrates Vera's sensuality, her life force.[12]

To my knowledge, there is only one psychoanalytic interpretation of the film. In a section called 'Between Joy and Suicide: Fathers, Daughters, and *Little Vera*', Horton and Brashinsky write of the film as depicting 'the raw edges ... of an Oedipal and patriarchal system (political, economic, cultural) of signification and representation that are showing serious signs of disruption and change'.[13] The Elektra complex would normally consider the daughter's admiration of her successful father. However, as these two critics see it, the problem here is that Vera's father is not the typical father figure. He has not made anything of himself. The film explores this unusual situation, 'the possibility of nurturing relationships between an "unsuccessful" and basically non-domineering father figure and daughter. [It] chart[s] this young Soviet woman's movement away from her father and towards her fiancé.'[14] Whether Vera will succeed is, of course, left open at the end of the film.

The Actors' Response
Natalia Negoda (Vera)
'I got a call from the Gorky studios, offering me a script. I read it. Well, I thought, there's an awful lot here! An attempted murder. A suicide attempt. Love. Blood. Laughter and tears.'

'We live in cynical times. Everything has become devalued. Prices rise but values fall.'

'Everyone is unhappy in his or her own way. You can have many friends and yet still not be understood by them. You can be married and still feel incredibly lonely.'[15]

Andrei Sokolov (Sergei)
'I warmed to the script immediately. Natalia Negoda grew up in an environment, in a family connected with art and the theatre. Whereas everything the scriptwriter wrote about was familiar to me. Like Sergei, I studied at a technical college. We're the same age. His life and mine almost overlapped. That's why I understand my character really well.'

'Sergei is more complex and brighter than Vera. He's been given much more. He ought to give something back. But my character is a representative of that tragic generation which no one needed. He wastes all his energy on enjoying himself. He reels in this girl. He puts on idiotic trousers and sets off to meet her parents. Of course he doesn't love her. It's just a bit of fun.'

'I really don't know if there is hope at the end. At any rate, it's not a happy ending. I imagine that the relationship between Vera and Sergei will be so tortuous and complicated that we'd need to make another film, *Little Vera II*, as they do with hits in the West.'[16]

Liudmila Zaitseva (Rita)
'The film is a confession ... It's about you and me, about how society could allow a lack of spiritual values to grow apace and stifle moral imperatives.'

'To be honest, when I read the script, I was antagonistic ... I thought here are young people who have come to film without having had any experience of real life and who have decided "to blacken" simple, normal, working people ... I decided not to take part in the film. But Vasili Pichul and I met ... The main thing I got from this meeting was that ... their only aim was to speak articulately and honestly about the main institution in our life, which unfortunately over the last few decades we have begun to neglect. This is the cell of society, the family. It isn't a personal story. It's our society in cross-section. We are not used to seeing on the screen the hard truth about ourselves. I appreciate that it shocked a lot of people, even though they were fully aware of the lack of spiritual values ... Indifference set in and, closing our eyes to real reality – our way of life, family scandals, and stupidity – we tried in every way possible to conceal distorting attitudes. We were taught to keep our voices down, whereas here everything is up front, on display.'

'[My character] is unlike anything I've ever done before in film ... [Those who have seen the film] for some reason think that Rita is a negative character. I totally disagree. I feel sympathy for her because I see myself in her. I also see many women who have been denied a natural, normal life and who have had to be content with something else instead. As someone rightly observed, my character is one of those women "who instinctively defend their hearth, even though the fire has long since gone out".'[17]

Iuri Nazarov (Kolia)

'Today we have somehow become very skilful at living with mutually exclusive concepts and situations. At some official meeting we vote, in all sincerity ... for reciprocity and détente in the world and at home squabble and bicker with our wives ... frequently in the presence of the children. At meetings and even in ordinary conversations in the kitchen, on the train or on the phone, we express so many wonderful and sound notions about education, hard work, honesty and conscientiousness. And at the same time we get our children into higher education by giving bribes or "gifts" ... Today the aims of the individual outweigh those of society. And what about after the War? Yes, we had the swine, the individualist, the one with no conscience, the one who dreamed only about his own prosperity when the whole country was doing its damnedest to drag itself out of the ruins! [By] watering down the aims of society and legitimising those of the individual, I think we forfeited a lot. Despite our guilty conscience we simply went on repeating the high-sounding words and saying that young people ... had somehow become allergic to them. And not only to these high-sounding words but to words of reason, too. It is we adults who are to blame.'[18]

Notes

1. *Sovetskii ekran*, no. 8 (1989), pp. 5–7.
2. *Sovetskii fil'm*, no. 6 (1989), p. 14.
3. Herbert Eagle, 'The Indexicality of *Little Vera* and the End of Socialist Realism', *Wide Angle*, 12, no. 4 (October 1990), p. 27.
4. *Sovetskii ekran*, no. 2, pp. 18–19; Maria Khmelik, *Little Vera*, London, 1990, pp. 121, 124, 129.
5. Hedrick Smith, *The New Russians*, London, 1990, pp. 111–12.
6. Lynne Attwood, *Red Women on the Silver Screen*, London, 1993, p. 112.
7. Anna Lawton, *Kinoglasnost: Soviet Cinema in Our Time*, Cambridge, 1992, p. 192.
8. *Iskusstvo kino*, no. 9 (1988), pp. 42–55.
9. *Dumaite o reklame*, 4, Moscow 'Soiuzinformkino' (1988), p. 25. The section devoted to *Little Vera* can be found on pp. 24–37.
10. *Monthly Film Bulletin*, 56 (July 1989), p. 195.
11. Marina Drozdova, 'Sublimations from Socialism', in Attwood, *Red Women on the Silver Screen*, p. 203.
12. Tatiana Moskvina, 'Forward, singing!', in Andrew Horton and Michael Brashinsky, *Russian Critics on the Cinema of Glasnost*, pp. 105–7.
13. Andrew Horton and Michael Brashinsky: *The Zero Hour: Glasnost and Soviet Cinema in Transition*, Princeton, NJ, 1992, p. 112.
14. Ibid., p. 113.
15. E. Karaeva, 'Zvezdnyi bilet Natashi Negody' [Natasha Negoda's ticket to the stars], *Sovetskii ekran*, no. 8 (1989) p. 11.
16. 'Zhenikh malenkoi Very' [Little Vera's fiancé], *Sovetskaia kultura*, 28 (October 1989) p. 5.
17. 'Ia ne Dzhul'etta' [I am no Juliet], *Ekran 90*, Moscow, 1990, pp. 113–14.
18. Interview with Iuri Nazarov, *Sovetskii ekran*, no. 4 (1989), pp. 24–5.

6. Concluding Remarks

We have followed closely the trials and tribulations of a Soviet, working-class family in this film. The impression we receive is not that of the model Soviet family so beloved by the state. We have seen how the members of this family bicker and yell at each other. The father fails to live up to the image of the glorious Soviet worker. He seeks solace in alcohol. His wife represents the lot of many working-class women in the Soviet Union, having to cope with the double burden of shift work and household chores and her husband's alcoholism. Vera is hardly the dutiful daughter. The son's marriage is on the rocks. Vera's prospects are limited. We have followed Vera's private story over the summer months. We have become acquainted with her friends, Andriusha, Lena and Tolik, and seen how they occupy their time in activities which are frowned upon by the state. We have suggested that the town and the authorities have 'failed' these young people, turning them into disillusioned and cynical beings. When it comes to relationships, these same young people do not really have any role models. Vera's parents had had Vera just to get a bigger flat! Andriusha's privileged parents have indulged him. Lena's mother's several failed relationships probably explain why Lena eventually settles for the dull, patriarchal but safe Mikhail Petrovich. We learn nothing of Tolik's family. The lack of parental guidance may well explain his becoming involved in criminal activities. In the meantime Vera gets to know Sergei, whose parents are privileged and materialistic. It is the consequences of embarking on this relationship which

Concluding Remarks 109

take up most of the film's narrative. Tolik eventually disappears from the scene. Any further friendship with Andriusha becomes impossible after his attempted rape. Once Lena marries Mikhail Petrovich, Vera will lose her best friend. Kolia, Rita and Viktor fail her, too. She feels so alienated that she thinks there is no way out except suicide. The film ends ambiguously. Although Vera does love Sergei, his feelings for her are less clear. We can only speculate about their future.

Little Vera is not a fully-fledged *glasnost* film; it is a transitional film. The spirit of *glasnost* allowed directors to look into some of the dark corners of Soviet society. *Little Vera* was a debut film. The fact that its director and scriptwriter were, and still are, married is important. 'Their tastes, their thoughts and aspirations complement one another to an uncommon degree.'[1] They have a sure touch. Vasili Pichul had first-hand knowledge of life in a pollution-soaked industrial town in the provinces, having been born in Zhdanov. His wife had also visited her husband's home town. She acknowledged the significance of the gender of the scriptwriter. As a young woman herself, she felt that she was in a position to describe Vera's point of view sympathetically, perhaps intuitively.[2]

The script was turned into a novel after the release of the film. It is well worth reading. The motivation of the characters is much clearer in the novel than in the film. For example, we are privy to much more information about Lena Chistiakova. Lena had taught Vera how to live and how to dress. Because money was tight at home, Lena had sold herself to foreign sailors down by the docks, once or twice a week. '"Doesn't it turn your stomach?' Vera had once asked her, and Chistiakova ... had said, "Of course it does. But what can a girl do if she needs money?" And Vera had known she was right. There were plenty of other girls doing it.'[3] Of Sergei we learn that he had entered the institute only to avoid military service and that he had used his good looks with the women lecturers, even having an affair with one whose husband was away at sea. As soon as he got a first-class mark from her, he dumped her. Furthermore, we learn more about his attitudes. After the confrontation between Sergei, Viktor and Vera in the hostel, Sergei begins to think that it is time to finish with Vera. They have had a bit of fun, it is now time to move on. We also learn that Sergei and Viktor first met during Viktor's summer break, two years before the events described in the film. They had arranged to sleep with the same girl on alternate nights. When Viktor returned to Moscow, Sergei had simply lost interest. Moreover, the reason why Viktor is married is starkly given: he wanted to obtain a permit to live in Moscow. Films and novels are, of course, predicated on selection, on a condensation of events and time. Although aware that film is a different medium, I feel that *Little Vera* might well have benefited from clearer character motivation. The viewer and the critic have to work hard and are often forced to resort to speculation.

In terms of cinematic technique, *Little Vera* deserves to be regarded as a success. It had been Pichul's intention to capture the essence of working-class *byt*. The use of a hand-held camera in the interior scenes is crucial. The characters almost collide with it or brush it aside. The cramped conditions are thus graphically portrayed. There are no 'tricksy' shots in this film. The majority of the shots are medium close-up or close-up, the more effectively to convey the changing relationships between the characters. Medium close-ups often turn into close-ups to pick out everyday objects, which anchor the film in a clearly defined environment. As for exterior locations, the favoured shot is either long or medium. The focus moves from the general to the more specific. The two panoramic shots which open and close the film act as a framing device. They serve to mark the parameters of this industrial, polluted town. Pichul's film is in colour, yet it works mainly because the colours are not Hollywood colours. These are the real colours of the industrial backwater where the film is set. A pall hangs over the town. Paradoxically, the pollution colours the town, though the effect is actually to 'discolour' it. The result is an authentic representation of grubby reality.

As befits a realist film, symbolism plays little part in its aesthetics. However, certain objects might profitably be viewed as having a symbolic value – the cardboard tiger, the train or the rain in the final shot, for instance, but they are also realistic details in their own right.

The film's success is due in no small part to the excellent ensemble acting. Two veteran actors, Liudmila Zaitseva and Nazarov, are placed opposite two newcomers, Natalia Negoda and Andrei Sokolov. The veterans' roles in *Little Vera* were a departure from the ones for which they were well known to Soviet film-goers. Zaitseva had carved out a career playing strong peasant women. Nazarov's forte had been

Concluding Remarks 111

playing square-jawed workers. Negoda had played one of the teenage pupils in Kara's *Tomorrow There was War* [Zavtra byla voina, 1987] and Sokolov had appeared in Babich's *Peasants!* [Muzhiki!, 1981] and Arkadi Kordon's *The Adventures of Travka* [Prikliuchenia Travki, 1976]. It requires a particular skill on the part of a director to get a disparate group of actors to gel. Pichul succeeded because he would listen as much as argue his point during filming.[4]

After *Little Vera*, Pichul left the Gorky Film Studios and set up his own independent production company called Gift [Podarok]. His first independent venture, *Dark Nights in Sochi* [Temnye nochi v Sochi, 1989], the screenplay of which had been written by his wife, flopped at the box-office, even though it starred Natalia Negoda. Husband and wife collaborated again on the 1993 film *The Dreams of an Idiot* [Mechty idiota], which brought together Andrei Sokolov, Nazarov and Zaitseva. It is loosely based on *The Golden Calf*, a brilliant satire written by Ilf and Petrov in 1931. Pichul, who on graduation had worked in television, returned to it in 1994 to produce, over the next four years, the satirical show *Puppets* [Kukly], the Soviet Union's answer to Britain's *Spitting Image*. Parody characterises Pichul's latest film *The Diamond-Studded Sky* [Nebo v almazakh, 1999], co-written with his wife. Maria Khmelik is currently running her own script-writing workshop at VGIK. Since *Little Vera*, Andrei Sokolov has directed in the theatre and has been in constant demand as an actor, both in films and televsion. He has worked with veteran directors and relative newcomers. For example he featured in Eldar Riazanov's *The Prophecy* [Predskazanie, 1994] and in Dmitri Astrakhan's TV series *The Waiting Room* [Zal ozhidania, 1998]. Sokolov has ambitions to direct films. Natalia Negoda was fêted after *Little Vera*, even appearing in *Playboy* as 'that *glasnost* girl', 'the Soviets' first sex star'. It is a label that she has found difficult to shake off. She played in American productions, for example, in 1992, opposite Roman Polanski and Brian Blessed in Deran Sarafian's disappointing *Back in the USSR* and in Tommy Lee Wallace's uninspired *The Comrades of Summer*, made for TV in 1992. In 1996 she was in Ulli Lommel's weird *Every Minute is Goodbye*.

Little Vera is often remembered for its frank portrayal of sex. As I hope I have shown, the film is much more significant than that. A

Soviet trailer for the film declared: 'A private story or the philosophy of stagnation which permeates everyday existence? The humdrum life of a good-time girl or a warning about a danger which concerns each and every one of us? Go and see *Little Vera*!'[5]

Little Vera is all of these. Go and see it (again)!

Notes

1. I. Dobrovolskaia, *Iskusstvo kino*, no. 7 (1989), p. 144.
2. Private conversation with the author.
3. Maria Khmelik, *Little Vera*, London, 1990, p. 13.
4. E. Karaeva, *Sovetskii ekran*, no. 8 (1989), p. 11.
5. Quoted in *Dumaite o reklame*, no. 4 (1988), p. 24.

Further Reading

General background
Lane, David, *Soviet Society under Perestroika*, London, 1992.
Shlapentokh, Vladimir, *Love, Marriage and Friendship in the Soviet Union*, New York, 1984.
Shlapentokh, Dmitry and Vladimir, *Soviet Cinematography 1918–1991. Ideological Conflict and Social Reality*, New York, 1993.
Wilson, Andrew and Nina Bachkatov, *Living with Glasnost. Youth and Society in a Changing Russia*, London, 1988.

Books which discuss the film
Attwood, Lynne, *Red Women on the Silver Screen: Soviet Women and Cinema from the Beginning to the End of the Communist Era*, London, 1993, pp. 111–13, 113–15, 202–3.
Galichenko, Nicholas, *Glasnost – Soviet Cinema Responds*, Austin, TX, 1991, pp. 110–11.
Horton, Andrew and Michael Brashinsky, *The Zero Hour: Glasnost and Soviet Cinema in Transition*, Princeton, NJ, 1992, pp. 111–17.
Horton, Andrew and Michael Brashinsky, *Russian Critics on the Cinema of Glasnost*, Cambridge, 1994, pp. 103–7.
Lawton, Anna, *Kinoglasnost: Soviet Cinema in Our Time*, Cambridge, 1992, pp. 192–4.
Smith, Hedrick, *The New Russians*, London, 1990, pp. 111–12.

Reviews and articles in English
Corliss, Richard, 'Censors' Day Off', *Time International*, Special Issue – The New USSR, 10 April 1989, pp. 71–2.
Eagle, Herbert, 'The Indexicality of *Little Vera* and the End of Socialist Realism', *Wide Angle*, 12, no. 4 (1990), pp. 26–37.

Glaessner, Verina, 'Malenkaya Vera [Little Vera]', *Monthly Film Bulletin*, 56 (July 1989), p. 195.

Horton, Andrew, 'Little Vera', *Film Quarterly*, 13, no. 4 (Summer 1989), pp. 18–21.

Plakhov, Andrei, 'Soviet Cinema into the 90s', *Sight and Sound*, 58, no. 2 (Spring 1989), pp. 82–3.

Williamson, Anne, 'Rubles of the Game', *Film Comment*, January–February 1989, pp. 23–6.

Websites

Database of Russian Films, <http://www.agama.com/cinema/>.

International Movie Database, <http://uk.imdb.com>.